Classical Mythology

Captivating Stories of Greek and Roman Gods, Heroes, and Mythological Creatures

© Copyright 2018

All rights Reserved. No part of this book may be reproduced in any form without permission in writing from the author. Reviewers may quote brief passages in reviews.

Disclaimer: No part of this publication may be reproduced or transmitted in any form or by any means, mechanical or electronic, including photocopying or recording, or by any information storage and retrieval system, or transmitted by email without permission in writing from the publisher.

While all attempts have been made to verify the information provided in this publication, neither the author nor the publisher assumes any responsibility for errors, omissions or contrary interpretations of the subject matter herein.

This book is for entertainment purposes only. The views expressed are those of the author alone, and should not be taken as expert instruction or commands. The reader is responsible for his or her own actions.

Adherence to all applicable laws and regulations, including international, federal, state and local laws governing professional licensing, business practices, advertising and all other aspects of doing business in the US, Canada, UK or any other jurisdiction is the sole responsibility of the purchaser or reader.

Neither the author nor the publisher assumes any responsibility or liability whatsoever on the behalf of the purchaser or reader of these materials. Any perceived slight of any individual or organization is purely unintentional.

Free Bonus from Captivating History (Available for a Limited time)

Hi History Lovers!

Now you have a chance to join our exclusive history list so you can get your first history ebook for free as well as discounts and a potential to get more history books for free! Simply visit the link below to join.

Captivatinghistory.com/ebook

Also, make sure to follow us on:

Twitter: @Captivhistory

Facebook: Captivating History:@captivatinghistory

Contents

FREE BONUS FROM CAPTIVATING HISTORY (AVAILABLE FOR A LIMITED TIME) 5

PART 1: GREEK MYTHOLOGY 8

CAPTIVATING GREEK MYTHS OF GREEK GODS, GODDESSES, MONSTERS AND HEROES 8

INTRODUCTION 1

PART I 3

THE GOLDEN AGE OF THE TITANS 3
    THE CREATION OF THE TITANS 3
    THE BIRTH OF THE OLYMPIANS AND THE DOWNFALL OF THE TITANS 4
    PROMETHEUS AND EPIMETHEUS 6
    THE BIRTH OF THE MUSES 8

PART II 10

THE OLYMPIAN GODS AND GODDESSES 10
    HERA, QUEEN OF THE GODS 10
    HERMES, TRICKSTER, AND MESSENGER OF THE GODS 11
    GREY-EYED ATHENA, GODDESS OF WISDOM AND STRATEGY 12
    HEPHAESTUS, GOD OF FIRE AND SMITHCRAFT 13
    ARTEMIS, VIRGIN GODDESS OF THE HUNT 14
    APOLLO, GOD OF MUSIC AND HEALING 14
    DIONYSUS, GOD OF WINE AND RITUAL MADNESS 16
    ARES, GOD OF WAR, AND APHRODITE, GODDESS OF LOVE 17
    THE STORY OF DEMETER AND PERSEPHONE 19

PART III 20

DEMIGODS, HEROES, AND MONSTERS 20
    THE STORY OF PERSEUS 20
    HERACLES 23
        The First Labor: The Nemean Lion 25
        The Second Labor: The Lernean Hydra 26
        The Third Labor: The Ceryneian Hind 27
        The Fourth Labor: The Erymanthian Boar 28
        The Fifth Labor: The Augean Stables 29
        The Sixth Labor: The Stymphalian Birds 30
        The Seventh Labor: The Cretan Bull 30
        The Eighth Labor: The Mares of Diomedes 32
        The Ninth Labor: The Belt of Hippolyta 32
        The Tenth Labor: The Cattle of Geryon 32
        The Eleventh Labor: The Golden Apples of the Hesperides 33

The Twelfth Labor: Cerberus, Dog of the Underworld 34
THESEUS AND THE MINOTAUR 36

PART 2: ROMAN MYTHOLOGY 39

A CAPTIVATING GUIDE TO ROMAN GODS, GODDESSES, AND MYTHOLOGICAL CREATURES 39

INTRODUCTION 40
THE SHAPE OF THINGS TO COME 40

CHAPTER 1 — THE TROJAN CONNECTION 42
WHAT HISTORY AND AN ANALYSIS OF MYTH TELL US 49

CHAPTER 2 — FOUNDING OF ROME 51
FROM THE SHE-WOLF TO THE FOUNDING OF A GREAT CITY 57

CHAPTER 3 — PURELY ROMAN GODS 58

CHAPTER 4 — BORROWINGS FROM ETRURIA 64
FROM RASENNA 66

CHAPTER 5 — INFLUENCE OF THE GREEK PANTHEON 67
FROM THE GREEKS 68
LESSER GODS AND GODDESSES 70
GREEK CREATURES ADOPTED BY THE ROMANS 71

CHAPTER 6 — CELTIC POTPOURRI 74
ROMAN CONQUESTS OF THE CELTS 75
OTHER BORROWED GODS 80

CHAPTER 7 — TRUTH BEHIND THE ROMAN GODS 82

CONCLUSION - WHAT WE'VE LEARNED 85

PREVIEW OF NORSE MYTHOLOGY 87

A CAPTIVATING GUIDE TO NORSE FOLKLORE INCLUDING FAIRY TALES, LEGENDS, SAGAS AND MYTHS OF THE NORSE GODS AND HEROES 87

BIBLIOGRAPHY 95

FREE BONUS FROM CAPTIVATING HISTORY (AVAILABLE FOR A LIMITED TIME) 96

Part 1: Greek Mythology

Captivating Greek Myths of Greek Gods, Goddesses, Monsters and Heroes

Introduction

Giants. Gods. Heroes. Monsters. These are the stuff of Greek myths and legends. These ancient stories tell the tales of the before-time, when the heavens and the earth were new, and when great deeds were done by beings who were larger than life.

The ancient Greeks had no concept of a unitary creator-god or set of creator-gods. For the ancient Greeks, the world simply came into being out of Nothingness. But for the Greeks, that Nothingness was in itself a being: the name of the first primordial god, Chaos, in fact, means "Chasm" or "Abyss," and into this abyss Mother Earth also came into being, unmade and unassisted. Greek creation myths also differ from those of for example the book of Genesis in that it's not only plants and animals that come into being through the actions of the gods. Things like Night, Death, Sleep, and Memory also were considered sentient beings that had their places in the ladder of creation and that deserved respect—if not worship—of mortal humans.

In addition to explaining how creation itself began, myths in many cultures have the function of "just-so" stories, explaining various other important things—the invention of fire, why we have weather, the names of plants and birds. Greek mythology is no different: enfolded in grand stories of gods and heroes are some of the ways the ancient Greeks understood many of the more common aspects of their world.

The world was a dangerous place for the ancient Greeks. Disease and famine, war and death were always around the corner and waiting to strike when one least expected it. The ancient Greeks thought that misfortune was the result of the caprice of the gods. Therefore, these myths also function as cautionary tales, warning humans of the sin of hubris, telling them to be humble and worship the gods as was just and right, so that maybe the gods would smile and take pity on the mortals they ruled.

Although the gods and goddesses were powerful immortal beings, they were in many ways still very like the humans who worshiped them and who created these tales. The gods and goddesses are stricken with jealousy; they fall in love; they get angry when they feel slighted, and bestow gifts when they are honored. Likewise, the heroes are larger than life: they're stronger, faster, and more skilled than ordinary mortals, but they are still subject to pain, illness, and death.

There are usually several different versions of these myths, which were told and retold over a span of many centuries. The versions presented here are an amalgamation from various ancient Greek sources. My goal has not been to create an "official" text, so sometimes I have mingled variants from different sources to create a single compelling narrative that at the same time is faithful to ancient ways of remembering these stories, which still have so much to tell us even today.

Part I
The Golden Age of the Titans

The Creation of the Titans

In the beginning, there was only Chaos. Out of Chaos came Darkness and Night. Night was mother to both Air and Day, but also to Doom, Death, Sleep, and Old Age, and many other children besides, and Darkness was their father.

After Chaos came Gaia, who is Mother Earth, and then Eros, the god of love. Gaia herself brought forth Uranus, that is Father Sky, and with him, Gaia made the first and oldest gods, the Titans, who governed the universe and peopled it with their divine children. Some of these children were fair beings, who themselves gave birth to gods and goddesses, but others were fearsome to behold. These were the Cyclops, great giants with only one eye each, and the Hecatoncheires, the Hundred-Handed Ones, three brothers with fifty heads and one hundred arms each. Father Sky feared the Cyclops and the Hecatoncheires. He captured them and imprisoned them in Tartarus, a terrible, dark cavern deep under the earth, from which nothing could escape.

Besides the Cyclops and Hundred-Handed Ones, together Mother Earth and Father Sky had twelve children, six males, who were Oceanus, Hyperion, Coeus, Cronus, Crius, and Iapetus; and six females, Mnemosyne (Memory), Tethys, Theia, Phoebe, Rhea, and Themis.

Uranus was jealous of his children and hid them away in a cavern deep inside Gaia. As Uranus put each child inside their mother, Gaia began to feel the pain of over-fullness, so she went and created a great sickle of adamant, the hardest of all metals, and showed it to her children.

"Which of you will take this sickle, and free us from Father Sky's oppression?" said Mother Earth.

But Gaia's children were all terrified of their father, and none would step forward to take the sickle, until one day Cronus said, "Give me the sickle, Mother. I will do as you ask."

Gaia hid Cronus away where Uranus would not see him and told him what he should do. As the day ended, Father Sky came to Mother Earth, covering her with night and wanting to make love to her. And when Uranus was stretched out over the fair Earth, Cronus took the sickle of adamant and cut his father's genitals off. Cronus cast these away behind him. Drops of Uranus' blood landed on Gaia and were taken into her, and from these were made the Furies, Alecto, Tisiphone, and Magaera, the goddesses of vengeance; and the Giants; and the nymphs of the trees.

Uranus' genitals landed in the ocean. As they floated on the water, white foam began to grow around them. The white foam grew and took the shape of a young woman, the purest and most beautiful of all. She stepped out of the water onto the island of Cyprus and is called Aphrodite, the goddess of love. Aphrodite had two helpers at her birth: Eros, the god of love, and Himeros, god of desire, who was born with her.

Once the Titans were all freed from the cavern, they took one another as husbands and wives and began to make children of their own. The Sun, Moon, and the Dawn were all children of Hyperion and Theia. Oceanus, the great sea that encircles the whole world, and his wife Tethys, were the parents of many mighty rivers, including the Nile and the Danube, and of Metis, the first wife of Zeus and mother of Athena, goddess of wisdom. Atlas, who holds the sky on his shoulders, and Prometheus, bringer of fire, and ill-fated Epimetheus were the sons of Iapetus and Asia, who herself was an Oceanid, a daughter of Oceanus and Tethys. Many of these Titans and children of Titans have stories of their own, some of which will be told later.

The Birth of the Olympians and the Downfall of the Titans

By far the most important descendants of the Titans were the Olympians, children of Rhea and Cronus, who eventually overthrew the older gods and came to rule over all creation from the heights of Mount Olympus, with Father Zeus at their head. And this is how that came to pass.

Rhea and Cronus, Titans both and children of Mother Earth and Father Sky, lived as husband and wife, and Rhea bore Cronus many children. But Cronus was jealous and grasping and had heard his reign over all that was would be ended by one of his children. Every time Rhea bore him a child, Cronus snatched it away and ate it, first Hestia, then Demeter, Hera, Hades, and Poseidon, one after the other, thinking that would protect him and secure his throne forever.

This made Rhea deeply sorrowful, so the next time she felt herself with child, she begged her parents, Mother Earth and Father Sky, for help. They agreed to help her, guiding her to a cave on the island of Crete, where Zeus was born and where Rhea hid her son far, far away within Gaia. There Zeus lived, cared for by his grandmother until he was grown.

After Rhea left Zeus in the cave, she swaddled a rock to make it look like a baby, and brought it to Cronus, saying, "See, here is your new-born son."

Cronus was so hasty in his jealousy and fear he swallowed the rock whole, without even looking at it. Then he was satisfied, thinking that he could never be overthrown since he had imprisoned every one of his children inside himself.

Meanwhile, in the cave on the island of Crete, Zeus grew in stature and might, and when he deemed the time was right, he left the cave and went searching for his father. He found mighty Cronus, and they had a fierce battle. Zeus was too strong for wicked Cronus and forced him to vomit up all his brothers and sisters. The first thing Cronus vomited up was the rock he had swallowed in Zeus' place. Then out came Poseidon, Hades, Hera, Demeter, and Hestia, one after the other. The rock Zeus kept, as a memorial to his victory, and had it placed in Pytho, on holy Mount Parnassus.

It became clear to Zeus that something needed to be done about who wielded power in the universe. Was it to be the old gods, the Titans? Or was it to be the younger gods and goddesses, the Olympians, who were his brothers and sisters? Clearly the Titans were not to be trusted: Zeus' father had eaten his children, after all, and Zeus had escaped that fate himself only through the courage and resourcefulness of his mother. Zeus knew he was strong, and so were his brothers and sisters, but he also knew he would need help. The first ones he decided to call upon were the Cyclops, terrible, one-eyed giants named Brontes (Thunderer), Steropes (Lightning), and Arges (Brightness), all of whom were gifted makers and smiths.

Now, the Cyclops had been imprisoned in Tartarus, a terrible, dark cavern far below the earth, from which there was no escape. Uranus, Father Sky, had placed them there for the first time, long ago, and there they stayed, until Cronus, father of the Olympian gods, freed them and asked them to help him overthrow Uranus. The Cyclops helped Cronus with a good will, and Uranus was overthrown, but wicked Cronus double-crossed the Cyclops: as soon as they were no longer of any use to him, he imprisoned them in Tartarus once again.

Zeus braved the terrible deeps of Tartarus and freed the Cyclops from their prison. In thanks for their freedom, they made thunder and lightning and gave these to Zeus, which he could then use in his battles with the Titans or whenever else he might have need of them. The Cyclops also bestowed a trident upon Poseidon and gave a helmet to Hades.

The Cyclops were not the only ones who Zeus freed from Tartarus. The Hecatoncheires, the Hundred-Handed Ones, Cottus (Furious), Briareus (Vigorous), and Gyges (Big-Limbed) were three sons of Uranus, and their mother was Gaia. These brothers each had fifty heads and a hundred arms and were fearsomely strong and brave in battle. These three brothers also had been imprisoned in Tartarus by Father Sky, and it was Rhea, mother of Zeus, who gave her son the idea to free these three brothers also, saying that if Zeus released them, he could call upon them for help when he needed it. Zeus followed his mother's advice. He descended again into the pit of Tartarus and freed the Hundred-Handed Ones who, as Rhea had said, then promised to fight for Zeus whenever he called.

With the weapons of the Cyclops and the help of the Hundred-Handed Ones, Zeus and the Olympians went to war against the Titans. There was a mighty battle, and in the end, the Titans were defeated. Zeus then imprisoned them in Tartarus and set the Hundred-Handed Ones to guard them. The next thing to be done was to divide up the rule of the universe. Zeus, the god of thunder and lightning, took the sky. Poseidon, the god of the sea, took the oceans and seas, and Hades was allotted the Underworld, the place of the Dead which also bears his name.

Prometheus and Epimetheus

Prometheus was the son of the Titan Iapetus and Clymene, daughter of Oceanus and Tethys, and Epimetheus was his brother. Prometheus fought on the side of the Olympians during their struggle against the Titans, and so never was imprisoned in Tartarus. Some say that Prometheus was the creator of mankind, fashioning human beings out of mud alongside his brother, Epimetheus and that they also made the animals, birds, and fish.

The brothers worked together to shape all the beasts and birds and fish. Epimetheus gave to them various gifts: feathers or fur; flight or crawling upon the earth; strength, swiftness, wisdom. When the creatures were all shaped and given their gifts, Athena breathed life into them. But when it came time for Prometheus to make humans, he found that Epimetheus had already given all the good things to the other animals, and the only things left to give the humans were the ability to walk upright, just as the gods and goddesses themselves did, and the gift of fire.

Prometheus loved the humans more than anything else, and although he had fought with the Olympians against the Titans, he was still angry with Zeus for imprisoning his family in the horrible pit of Tartarus. One day, as Prometheus thought to teach the humans how to make sacrifice to great Zeus, and to teach that mighty god a lesson. The humans sacrificed a bull to Zeus, and Prometheus told them to make two piles, one with the bones covered by a mound of fat, and the other with the choice parts of the meat wrapped up in the animal's hide. Prometheus told Zeus, "You can have first choice, but that will be what you accept from the humans for the rest of time."

Zeus suspected a trick, but he agreed to Prometheus' conditions. He looked at the two portions, one that was a lump covered in hide, the other a mound of luscious fat. Zeus took the portion with the fat but was enraged when he found that underneath it was no meat, but just a pile of bones. Even though he was very angry, Zeus kept his word, and from then on when humans made sacrifice to him, they gave him the fat and the bones, and he accepted that from them.

However, Zeus felt he could not let that trick go unpunished: he took fire away from the humans. The poor humans shivered in their homes, unable to warm themselves and growing thin because they could not cook their food. Prometheus took pity on them and decided to give fire back to them, no matter what Zeus might think or do. Prometheus took a great torch and lit it by holding it against the sun. He then brought the fire back to the humans, who rejoiced that they could once again warm their homes and cook their food and do all the other many things they needed fire to do.

Zeus saw this and decided to punish both Prometheus and humankind. But that wasn't the only reason he was angry with Prometheus: Prometheus had also said that one of Zeus' children would overthrow him and refused to say who it would be. In order to punish Prometheus, first Zeus ordered two of his servants, Violence, and Authority, to go with the smith-god Hephaestus to take Prometheus and chain him to a great rock in the Caucasus Mountains with a diamond chain that not even the son of a Titan could break. Then Zeus sent a giant eagle to eat Prometheus' liver every day. Since Prometheus was an immortal god, his liver grew back every time afterward, and so he suffered and could not die.

Zeus said that he would let Prometheus go if either he told Zeus who would dethrone him, or if a mortal offered to die in his place. Some say that Prometheus eventually was set free when the centaur Chiron agreed to die for Prometheus and the mighty hero Heracles helped set him free by capturing the eagle and killing it, and by breaking the chains. But Prometheus never told Zeus who it was that would overthrow him: that secret he kept forever.

The great god Zeus never got over his shame at Prometheus' trick with the bones and the fat, nor of his jealousy over humans getting fire back. Once Zeus had bound Prometheus to his rock and set upon him the eagle, he next turned his attention to Prometheus' brother, Epimetheus, who had helped in the creation of the humans who had helped Prometheus work mighty Zeus' humiliation at the sacrifice. If Prometheus and his humans could play a trick on Zeus, then Zeus could do the same to Epimetheus, and Zeus went about it this way: first, he went to Hephaestus and told him to make a human woman more beautiful than any other on earth. Then Zeus took the woman to Hermes, and told him to make her untrustworthy, and to make her a liar. They called this woman Pandora. Zeus also gave Pandora a box that she was told she must never, ever open.

Zeus took Pandora down to the Earth, where Epimetheus had been living among the humans. Zeus gave Pandora to Epimetheus as a gift. Epimetheus remembered that his brother had told him not to trust Zeus, and never to accept any gifts from him, but Pandora was so beautiful Epimetheus couldn't help himself: he accepted her gladly and took her to be his wife.

For a time, Pandora and Epimetheus lived happily together, but the mysterious box preyed on Pandora's mind. She wondered repeatedly what was inside it. What if she took just a little peek? What if she opened the box only the very tiniest crack? Surely nothing bad would come of that.

Pandora thought about it and thought about it. She couldn't banish thoughts of the box from her head. So, one day, when Epimetheus had gone out, she took the box down from its shelf. She set it on a table and very slowly, very carefully, she opened it the tiniest of cracks. But her care in opening it didn't matter: the box was filled with all the evils of the world—Fear, Disease, Hunger, Pain, Envy, Spite, and all manner of other foul things—and they were so numerous and so strong that they pushed the lid wide open and escaped out into the world to plague mankind. Pandora closed the box as quickly as she could, but not before all the things had escaped except one: Hope. And that is why humans still have hope, even in a world that is full of death and sickness and woe.

The Birth of the Muses

One time Zeus saw Mnemosyne, Titan daughter of Mother Earth and Father Sky, and he desired her greatly. So, Zeus came to her once a night for nine nights, and soon she found herself pregnant. When her time came, Mnemosyne gave birth to nine beautiful daughters. These daughters grew up to be beautiful women, skilled in many arts, and they are the ones that humans call on for help when they wish for inspiration, and they are known together as the Muses.

Calliope was the eldest, and it is she who encourages men to write tales of gods and heroes and to sing of great deeds. Clio is the Muse of history, of the telling of true stories of kings and empires, while Euterpe helps men write music and lyric poetry. When a man is in love and wants to write a poem for his beloved, he calls upon Erato, whose skill is in the verse of love, while dramatists call on Melponeme for tragedy and Thalia for comedy. Polyhmnia gives humans the ability to write good songs in praise of the almighty gods, while Terpsichore teaches them to dance with grace and joy. And finally, Urania is the Muse of astronomy, helping humans to learn and understand the motions of the heavens and what these mean to people on Earth.

It may seem odd to us today to consider the study of astronomy among all these other literary and musical arts, but it wouldn't have been seen this way by people in ancient Greece. Whereas we think of things like "melody" as the tune of a musical piece, and of "harmony" as musical chords or adding a second voice part to a melody, the ancient Greeks had a much broader and more complex understanding of those terms that went far beyond things like songs or instrumental music. The ancient Greek concept of "melos" (which is where we get our word "melody") encompassed the text, the rhythm, and sometimes even the dance movements that went along with a particular piece. And "harmony" wasn't just a pleasing way of making chords or having different musical lines work with each other: it also encompassed the idea of proper relationships among human beings, and between human beings and the universe at large.

This concept of connections between music and the structure of society and the universe was so powerful that it led many philosophers to suppose that the structure of the universe was itself musical. The idea that each planet creates its own kind of musical hum, and that these hums can be expressed as musical intervals from one planet to the other, is often attributed to the Greek mathematician Pythagoras and was an accepted way of understanding the universe well into the Renaissance.

For one of the Muses to be associated with the study of the heavens and the structure of the universe, while her sisters all deal in music and poetry of different kinds, is therefore not surprising. The harmony of the universe and the place of humans within it was just as much a musical thing to ancient people as the songs they sang or tunes they danced to.

Part II
The Olympian Gods and Goddesses

We have heard much of the deeds of Father Zeus, how he defeated the Titans and chained Prometheus, and did many other mighty things. Now we turn our thoughts to the other Olympian gods, the siblings and children of great Zeus.

Hera, Queen of the Gods

Hera was the daughter of Rhea and Cronus, the third wife of mighty Father Zeus, goddess of women, of marriage, and of the sky. Hera bore Zeus three children, of whom the most famous was violent Ares, god of war. She was the foster-daughter of Tethys, who cared for her at the time that Zeus and his brothers were fighting the Titans. Some say that when the battle with the Titans was done, Hera, Poseidon, and Hades became afraid of Zeus in his great power and tried to chain him. He was set free when Thetys went to Briareus, one of the Hundred-Handed Ones, who came to Olympus and stood by Zeus' side. After that, the other gods didn't dare try to chain Zeus again.

Zeus had already had several wives and fathered many children by the time he married Hera, and his wandering ways did not stop once they were wed. Hera suffered much from the infidelities of Zeus. Her jealousy led her to create a son of her own, crafty Hephaestus, and she often tried to destroy Zeus' other children, even that greatest of heroes and her namesake, the mighty Heracles himself.

Hera was not without her admirers, although she did not welcome them. The story is told of a man named Ixion, who desired Hera and pressed his attention on her. Hera did not want this, and so told Zeus. Zeus then tricked Ixion by presenting him with a cloud made into Hera's likeness. Ixion thought this was Hera and so made love to it. Some say that from Ixion's union with the cloud was born the first centaur. But even though Ixion had not slept with Hera herself, his presumption could not go unpunished. Zeus therefore fixed him to a wheel and doomed him to go spinning through the air, pushed by the winds, for all eternity.

Hermes, Trickster, and Messenger of the Gods

Atlas was the son of Iapetus and brother of Prometheus, and his wife was Pleione, daughter of Ocean. Together they had seven daughters, the Pleiades, one of whom was named Maia. Zeus looked upon Maia and desired her, and so he made love to her. Soon she became pregnant and gave birth to a baby boy, whom she named Hermes.

Now, Hermes was a precocious lad, and even when he was an infant, he started playing tricks. The first trick he played was on the god Apollo. Hermes left the cave where he had been living with his mother and went to Pieria where he stole a herd of cattle belonging to the elder god. To cover his tracks, he put shoes on the feet of the cattle to confuse their tracks. Hermes took the cattle to Pylus, where he sacrificed some of them, then ate some of the flesh and burned the rest. The cattle he did not sacrifice he hid inside a cave.

When he had finished this deed, he sat for a while outside the cave. After a time, he noticed a tortoise making its slow way across the grass. Hermes caught the tortoise and killed it. He scraped out the inside of its shell and put strings across it. In this way, Hermes invented the lyre. He also designed a plectrum to use to play it.

Meanwhile, Apollo learned of Hermes' theft of his cattle, and he went looking for the young god so he could get them back. He went to Hermes' mother and accused her son of stealing the cattle. But Maia held up the infant Hermes and said, "How could this small baby have stolen a herd of cattle?"

But Apollo wasn't fooled. He took Hermes before Zeus and told him about the theft of the cattle. At first, Hermes denied he had the animals, but eventually, he relented and took Apollo to the cave where he had hidden them. The lyre Hermes had made was at the cave, too. Apollo asked what it was, so Hermes showed him how to play it. Apollo was entranced by this new instrument, so he gave the cattle to Hermes in exchange for it, and that is how Apollo came to be a player of the lyre.

Hermes took the cattle to pasture and cared for them; now they were his own. But watching over the cattle sometimes was boring, so Hermes fashioned a flute for himself to play and thus while away the time. Apollo heard the flute and went to see what it was. There he found Hermes playing the shepherd's pipe. Apollo asked to have the pipe, but Hermes wouldn't give it to him for the asking: in exchange, he demanded Apollo's golden wand so he would then have the power of divination. Apollo thought it a fair exchange, so he got the flute and Hermes took the golden wand.

Zeus made Hermes his special messenger. Hermes also is the patron of trade, of cattle, and of tricksters.

Grey-Eyed Athena, Goddess of Wisdom and Strategy

Zeus' first wife was Metis, daughter of the Titans Oceanus and Tethys. Metis soon found herself pregnant by Zeus. Mother Earth and Father Sky warned Zeus she would bring forth a child so wise and mighty that he could overthrow his father. This made Zeus very worried. He asked Mother Earth and Father Sky for advice, and they told him he should swallow the child, as his father, Cronus, had done. Zeus decided he wouldn't wait until the child was born. He snatched up pregnant Metis and swallowed her whole.

Metis went up into Zeus' head and gave birth to a fine daughter. Metis then set about weaving a robe and making a helmet for her child. The incessant hammering on the helmet gave Zeus a mighty headache. Nothing he did could make it stop. In agony, he begged the other gods for help. Finally, great Prometheus took an ax and swung it right down the middle of Zeus' head, although some say that this was Hephaestus' doing. From the wound sprang a goddess, fully grown, dressed in a beautiful robe and armed with a helmet. This was Zeus' daughter, Athena, goddess of wisdom, justice, and strategy, and the city of Athens is named for her and under her particular protection, and this is how that came to be.

Once there was a king named Cecrops, and he founded a great city. Some say that Cecrops was not a human man, but rather had the upper body of a man and the tail of a great serpent or fish instead of legs. Some also say that Cecrops was the first one to offer sacrifice to Zeus and to declare him a god after the defeat of the Titans. Cecrops wanted a patron god or goddess for his city, so he offered to let the Olympians vie for that honor. Poseidon and Athena decided that they would enter the contest. Poseidon walked to the top of the Acropolis, the great stone hill in the center of the city and struck the ground with his great trident. A gush of pure, clear water came bubbling out, symbolizing that Poseidon could give Athens enormous power over the seas, and a mighty navy. Athena planted an olive tree, symbolizing peace and prosperity. Cecrops consulted with the people of the city as to which deity they wished as the patron of their city, and the people said, "We want Athena." And so, the city was named Athens, and the people took the goddess Athena to be their protectress, building her a fine temple atop the Acropolis.

Athena bestowed her favor on those who honored her, and destruction and disgrace on those who did not, but she always judged fairly. One story tells of a young man named Tiresias, whose mother was a nymph. One day, Tiresias came upon the goddess Athena where she was bathing. Tiresias hadn't meant to intrude, but the virgin goddess was angry that a man had seen her naked, and so struck Tiresias blind. Tiresias' mother vouched for her son and begged the goddess to restore his sight, but she could not do so. Instead, Athena cleaned his ears with a woolen cloth, after which

Tiresias could understand the speech of birds. With this understanding, Tiresias became a famous and mighty seer and prophet.

This goddess, wise in strategy, also favored those who work with skill and craft. Once there was a boy named Perdix who was an apprentice to the builder Daedalus. Perdix was a great observer of nature and tried to make useful things based on what he had seen. One day he looked at the backbone of a fish. Then he went and got a sheet of iron and cut teeth into one edge, in imitation of the ridges in the fish's spine. He discovered this edge could cut wood very easily: Perdix had invented the saw. But his master, Daedalus, was very jealous of his apprentice's talent. He seized Perdix and threw him over the edge of the Acropolis, but made it look like Perdix had fallen by accident. Athena saw the boy as he was falling, and rescued Perdix by turning him into a bird. Perdix even kept his own name afterward, since "Perdix" means "partridge."

Hephaestus, God of Fire and Smithcraft

When Hera saw Zeus had given birth to wise, grey-eyed Athena, she was jealous and vowed to get her own back by producing a child without the aid of either Zeus or any other. Soon Hera gave birth to a baby boy, whom she named Hephaestus. But Hera was disgusted by the child because its legs were shriveled. She therefore threw the young Hephaestus down from Olympus. But Eurynome, daughter of Oceanus, and Thetys, daughter of Nereus, caught the baby. They took him into their home, and there he began to show his great skill at working with metal, making all manner of weapons and armor and jewelry.

Hephaestus was angry that Hera had barred him from Olympus and vowed to find a way to rejoin the other gods. He therefore made a special chair that he sent up to Hera as a gift, but in fact the chair was cursed: anyone but Hera might sit in it and come to no harm, but if the Queen of Olympus sat in it, there she would be bound fast until Hephaestus saw fit to let her go.

The chair was brought up to Olympus, and soon enough Hera decided to sit in it. There she was caught fast. Some say that Zeus offered the hand of Aphrodite to the one who would release her, and this tale is told in the story of Ares, the God of War. Others say the other gods and goddesses went to Hephaestus and urged him to come to Olympus to set her free since she was his mother, and that Hephaestus refused until Dionysus got him drunk and brought him back to the abode of the gods. There Hephaestus released Hera from the cursed chair, and he was welcomed back into Olympus.

Hephaestus continued his metalworking even after his return to the abode of the gods, and he would make things for those who asked. Some things he made were good, such as the armor worn by Achilles when he went to fight on the shores of Troy; others he made caused suffering, such as the chains of Prometheus and the young woman Pandora, who released so many woes upon the world.

Artemis, Virgin Goddess of the Hunt

Leto was the daughter of the Titans Coeus and Phoebe. Zeus desired her and took her to be his wife. Soon Leto became pregnant with twins, a boy, and a girl. The boy she named Apollo and the girl she named Artemis.

Artemis loved wild animals, and she loved the hunt. Although many desired her, she had no wish to take a lover or to be married, so she went to Father Zeus and asked that she be permitted to remain a virgin forever. Artemis also asked of mighty Zeus a bow and arrows, a tunic that came to the knee so she could run and hunt, and the company of many nymphs who would be her friends and helpers, and who would care for her hunting dogs. Zeus loved Artemis greatly, and so granted her these wishes. Her bow and arrows were made by none other than the Cyclops, the great makers, and smiths who forge thunderbolts for mighty Zeus. The hounds of Artemis were no ordinary dogs: they were a gift of the god Pan, who gave her seven good dogs of his very own, swift to the hunt, and unafraid even of lions. Artemis also desired a chariot to take her to and fro, so she chased after five golden-antlered deer that were strong and tireless and as large as bulls. She was only able to capture four of them; the fifth escaped and ran into the Ceryneian hills and was only captured again when great Heracles did his mighty deeds.

Thus, Artemis became the protectress of wild animals and hunters, of young maidens and children. She also was sacred to women in childbirth, because it is said that when the time came for Leto to have her babies, Artemis was born first, and then helped her mother with the delivery of her brother.

Artemis jealously guarded her virginity, and let no male come near her, whether man or god. One day the hunter Actaeon came upon Artemis and her nymphs when they were bathing, and instead of turning away Actaeon decided to spy upon them. When Artemis caught him, she turned him into a deer and set his own dogs on him. The dogs hunted Actaeon, leaped upon him, and killed him, a punishment for his forwardness in gazing upon Artemis while she was naked.

Although Artemis never took either lover or husband, she did have male friends. One of these was Orion, a great hunter, and giant. Orion boasted he could kill any animal that walked upon the earth, no matter how fearsome. Mother Earth heard this and was angered. She sent a great scorpion to attack Orion. The scorpion stung him on the heel, and Orion died from the poison. Artemis grieved her friend's death and appealed to the Olympian gods to place him in the heavens. The gods heard her plea and put both Orion and the fatal scorpion in the sky as constellations.

Apollo, God of Music and Healing

Apollo was the son of Leto and mighty Zeus, and the twin brother of Artemis, goddess of the hunt. Like his sister, Apollo demanded a bow and arrows, but he also took up the lyre Hermes had made, so that he might make music and create songs. Apollo became the most accomplished musician among all the Olympians and the patron god of those who sing and play music. Apollo is the enforcer of Zeus' will, and it is his arrows that bring death and sickness to men when they disobey or anger the eternal gods, but he has equal power to heal and refresh, and sometimes will take away illness from those who beg his mercy and worship him with proper sacrifice.

The Oracle of Delphi was sacred to golden Apollo, and this is how it came to be his. Long, long ago, in the beginning of the world, Gaia, that is Mother Earth, came to Delphi. She saw that the place was sacred because this was where almighty Zeus had set the stone that Rhea tricked Cronos into swallowing in place of the infant Zeus. So, Mother Earth set a great serpent named Python to guard the stone from all who would trespass there.

Some say that Apollo was angry at Python because the serpent had chased his mother when she was pregnant with him; others say that he wanted access to the oracle, but Python would not let him pass. Either way, Apollo decided that Python was his enemy and needed to be destroyed, so he took his bow and shot her through with arrows. When the serpent was dead, Apollo took possession of the oracle, and from then on it was a place sacred to him.

Like Zeus, his father, Apollo sometimes fell in love with mortals. He was especially enamored of a young man named Hyacinth. Hyacinth was the most beautiful of all men, with a well-made body and thick, dark hair. One day, Apollo was practicing with the discus. His throw went wild, and struck Hyacinth in the head, killing him. Apollo was beside himself with grief for having slain the young man he loved so much. As a memorial to Hyacinth and his beauty, Apollo caused flowers to spring up in the places where Hyacinth's blood had flowed, and the flowers are still named after Apollo's beloved today.

Apollo could love very deeply, but he was also capable of great anger and cruelty. Apollo was jealous of his status as the greatest musician of all, as that satyr, Marsyas found out to his great misery, and this is how that came about. One day the goddess Athena desired to make some music, so she created a new instrument. It had two pipes with reeds in them, and it was played by blowing on the reeds and fingering the holes in the pipes. Athena was very pleased with her new instrument, which she called an *aulos,* and went about Olympus making music on it. But the other gods and goddesses laughed at her because of the way she puffed out her cheeks when she was playing it. This made Athena feel ashamed, so she threw the aulos away.

The satyr Marsyas chanced upon the aulos where Athena had thrown it. He picked it up and blew into it. He liked the sound it made, so he taught himself to play songs on it. Soon he was an accomplished musician, able to play many different melodies, and to play them very well. "Ha!" said Marsyas. "I am as good a musician as the great god Apollo himself!"

Apollo heard Marsyas' boast, and it made him angry. Apollo went to him and challenged him to a contest of musical skill. They agreed that the winner would be able to do whatever he wanted to the loser.

Apollo picked up his lyre and played, skillfully and well. Marsyas picked up his aulos and played, ably and well. For a long time, it seemed that neither of them would win. Until Apollo turned his lyre upside down and began to play on it. "Can you play your aulos upside down?" he asked Marsyas.

But Marsyas could not. Apollo was judged the winner of the contest, and the penalty he gave poor Marsyas was to be skinned alive.

Dionysus, God of Wine and Ritual Madness

Semele was the daughter of Cadmus and Harmonia. Zeus fell in love with her and took her to his bed, but he did so secretly, and in the dark, for she was human, and he did not want to hurt her by revealing his true self. Semele wanted to see Zeus in his full glory. She asked him to come to her in the same way he went to his divine wife, Hera. Zeus reluctantly agreed and came to her in thunder and lightning. This caused Semele to miscarry the baby she had by Zeus before she died of fright. Semele had only been six months along, and Zeus did not want the child to die as well, so he took the baby, who was named Dionysus, and sewed it into his thigh until it was old enough to be born. Thus, Dionysus is sometimes referred to as the "twice-born" god.

Zeus gave the baby to Hermes to care for, and Hermes brought him to his mother's sister, Ino, who was married to a man named Athamas. Some say that Hermes persuaded Ino and Athamas to bring Dionysus up as a girl, but that jealous Hera made them go insane, so Zeus rescued the child by turning him into a sheep and sending him to live with the nymphs of Nysa. Others say that Dionysus and his dead mother were placed in a chest, and when they washed up on shore, Ino found them. Ino and her people gave Semele a decent burial, and she brought up the child in safety.

Whatever his upbringing, it was Dionysus who discovered the grapevine and the way to make wine. Some say that Hera also threw Dionysus into a state of madness, out of jealousy over Zeus' dalliance with Semele and that this is why he wandered the world for many years. Dionysus went to Egypt and Syria, then to Phrygia and Thrace. Thrace was at war with India at the time, and Dionysus fought for the Thracians.

Next Dionysus went to Thebes, where he drove the women into a mad frenzy. The men of Thebes did not like this and tried to put a stop to it. Dionysus felt dishonored by this and commanded the women to attack the men. They did so, rending the men limb from limb. A similar thing happened at Argos: when the people there failed to do him honor, he made the women go mad, killing the men and their own infants in their delirium.

Dionysus had a mind to sail to Naxos, so he found a ship that would take them there. But the ship was manned by pirates who, not knowing that Dionysus was a god, conspired to sail to Asia instead and sell him as a slave. Dionysus learned what they were planning, so he turned the mast and oars into snakes and made ivy grow, and the sound of flutes play all over the ship. This drove the pirates mad. They all jumped overboard, and Dionysus turned them into dolphins. Dionysus eventually came to Naxos, where he found the young Ariadne sleeping, and he took her to be his wife, as is told in the story of the great hero Theseus.

Once Dionysus was done with his travels, wherever he went he was accompanied by a great throng of satyrs and wild, young girls called Maenads. And some say that before Dionysus went up into Olympus, he first went down to Hades to find his mother. When he found her, he changed her name to Thyone and brought her to Olympus with him.

Ares, God of War, and Aphrodite, Goddess of Love

Ares was the son of Zeus and Hera. A violent and changeable god, he loved battle and killing and sometimes switched his loyalties from one side to the other. This happened during the great war between Greece and Troy, that started upon the abduction of Helen. When the Trojan war began, Ares fought first on the side of the Greeks, but fair Aphrodite later convinced him to lend his might to the Trojans.

Warriors and those who excelled in the use of weapons were beloved of Ares, and he favored them with gifts. As is told in the tales of the great hero Heracles, to Hippolyta, queen of the Amazons, Ares gave a precious belt; to Diomedes, he gave fierce, flesh-eating horses.

Now, Ares loved the goddess Aphrodite, she who was born from the sea-foam, and she loved him, but they had not yet been bound as man and wife when the smith-god Hephaestus sent the cursed throne in which Queen Hera was bound. Some say that when Hera could not be freed by the efforts of any of the other Olympians, Father Zeus offered fair Aphrodite to be wife of whoever could free Hera. Aphrodite agreed, thinking that surely brave, strong Ares would be able to accomplish this. But nothing Ares did could free Hera from the chair. Finally, Hephaestus came to Olympus, and he freed Hera with ease.

As promised, Hephaestus was given Aphrodite to be his wife. Aphrodite was very unhappy with this. She didn't want to be the wife of crippled Hephaestus. So, one day, when Ares knew Hephaestus was out, he came to Aphrodite, and they went to bed together. They thought they were making love in secret, but Helios, the sun-god, saw them and told Hephaestus. Hephaestus was furious. He went to his forge and made a set of chains, woven in a strong net, with which to capture the lovers. The next time Ares and Aphrodite were together, Hephaestus came into the bedroom and threw the net over them. There the two lovers were trapped; they could not get away.

Hephaestus called all the other gods of Olympus to come and see the lovers' shame. They came, and they laughed at Ares and Aphrodite, all except Poseidon, who asked Hephaestus to let them go, saying that Ares would pay whatever price the smith-god asked. Hephaestus laughed. "Ares is not trustworthy, as you can see. I doubt he will pay a single penny."

But Poseidon insisted. He said that if Ares refused to make good his debt, that he would pay in his stead. So, Hephaestus let Ares and Aphrodite go, and they ran away to live in love on the island of Cyprus, the place where fair Aphrodite first arose from the sea.

Ares and Aphrodite had a daughter, Harmonia, who became the wife of King Cadmus of Illyria and mother to Semele, whom Zeus loved and who was the mother of the god Dionysus. When the Illyrians went to war, Ares fought for them, and Harmonia herself entered the fray among the soldiers, as a daughter of Ares should do.

Ares did not go into war unaccompanied. His charioteers Deimos (Terror) and Phobos (Fear) were ever with him, and some say that these also were children Ares had by Aphrodite. The goddess Eris (Strife), daughter of Night, was often said to be Ares' sister. She also goes with him into battle, making the hate and suffering of mankind even worse.

Aphrodite, the beloved of war-god Ares, was the goddess of love, but like all the Olympians she could become angry if she felt disrespected. Some say that anger at disrespect was the cause of the birth of the lovely youth, Adonis, and this is how that came about. King Thais of Assyria had a daughter, Smyrna, who refused to honor Aphrodite. As a punishment, Aphrodite made Smyrna desire her own father. Smyrna played a trick on Thais that allowed her to share his bed with him for twelve nights, but he was unaware that the woman he slept with was his daughter. When Thais learned how Smyrna had tricked him, he was angry and ashamed. He prayed to the gods that his daughter be punished for her crime, and they granted his wish by turning her into a myrrh tree, and indeed, this was fitting, for the name "Smyrna" means "myrrh."

But Smyrna was with child at the time of this punishment, so when the nine months had passed, the tree burst open and out came a beautiful baby boy, who was called Adonis. Aphrodite saw this and took Adonis to Persephone that he might be looked after, thinking she could get Adonis back later, except Persephone loved the boy and would not give him back when Aphrodite asked. The two goddesses brought the matter before Father Zeus for judgment. Zeus said that Adonis would spend part of the year with Persephone, part with Aphrodite, and part with himself. Adonis was later killed when he went hunting and was gored by the tusks of a boar. Some say that this was the work of Ares, who was jealous of Aphrodite's love for the young man; others say it was a punishment from Artemis because Adonis was such a fine hunter.

The Story of Demeter and Persephone

Persephone was the daughter of Demeter, goddess of the harvest, and Zeus was her father. Persephone was very beautiful, and many of the gods desired her. Apollo asked for her hand, as did Hermes, but Demeter refused them all and took Persephone away to a place where the gods could not find her.

Persephone loved growing things, especially flowers. One day, she was out gathering flowers with her maidens. Persephone especially loved the white narcissus for their delicate blooms and thick, sweet scent. She found a place in the meadow with an abundance of narcissus flowers, and she sat among them to gaze at their beauty.

Now, Hades, the Lord of the Underworld, also had wished to court Persephone but had been prevented by her mother. Hades knew of Persephone's love for the narcissus flower, and so had caused them to grow in that meadow, to lure her to that spot. So, while Persephone sat among the narcissus that Hades had planted, Hades jumped into his chariot that was pulled by many fine black horses. He thundered out of the Underworld and into the meadow, where he snatched up Persephone. Heedless of her cries, Hades drove his chariot back into the Land of the Dead, taking Persephone with him, thinking to make her his wife.

When Demeter learned her daughter had been taken, she searched all over the earth for her. So, stricken was she at the loss of Persephone she neglected the earth. The crops ceased to grow, and the trees ceased to bear fruit. A hard, lean time came for the people and the animals, a time of cold and harsh barrenness.

The people cried out to great Zeus for help, because they were starving. Even the other gods and goddesses begged him to intervene because the earth was no longer hospitable even to them, and the people who gave them worship were now too sick and weak to make sacrifice. Zeus therefore commanded Hades give Persephone back. The god of the Dead bowed to the will of almighty Zeus and agreed. He let Persephone go when Hermes arrived to take her back to the Land of the Living. But Hades first had played a trick on Persephone: he convinced her to eat three pomegranate seeds. Because Persephone had eaten the food of the Dead in the Land of the Dead, she was bound to that place for part of every year. When Persephone and her mother are reunited, the crops grow again, and the plants and trees are green, and the earth is warm and fertile. But every year for three months, Persephone goes back into the Underworld to live with Hades, one month for every pomegranate seed, and these are the months of winter when Persephone's absence makes Demeter sad, and the earth becomes cold and falls barren again for a time.

Part III
Demigods, Heroes, and Monsters

The Story of Perseus

Acrisius was king of Argos, and he had a beautiful daughter named Danae. But try as he might, he was unable to father a son. Acrisius asked an oracle what he needed to do to get a male heir, and the oracle replied by telling him that his daughter would bear a son, but the son would kill him. So Acrisius seized Danae and imprisoned her, thinking to prevent her from getting married and having children. But Father Zeus had seen Danae and desired her. One night Zeus came to Danae in the shape of a shower of gold. Danae found herself with child by him, and soon the child was born, a fine, strong boy. His mother gave him the name "Perseus."

When Acrisius found out that Danae had given birth to a son, he thought to rid himself of them both. He sealed mother and child into a chest and had the chest cast into the sea. The chest did not sink, but floated on the waves until it reached the island of Seriphus. A man named Dictys found the chest on the beach. He opened it and freed Danae and Perseus. Dictys took mother and son into his home, and he raised the boy as his own. Time passed, and Perseus grew into a fine figure of a man.

Now, Polydectes, the king of Seriphus and brother of Dictys, saw Danae and desired her, but he didn't dare touch her because Perseus was now a grown man and protected his mother. So Polydectes came up with a way to shame Perseus and get him out of the way so as to have Danae for himself. First Polydectes decided to throw a party to collect wedding gifts for his friend's daughter. Every guest was supposed to bring a gift of horses, but Perseus had no horses to give. Polydectes knew this, and he also knew that Perseus was honorable, brave, and strong, and these were things that could be used against him.

When Perseus appeared at the party, he apologized for not having horses to give. But he didn't want to dishonor either his host or the bridal couple, so he told Polydectes, "Name the gift, and I will get it for you."

Polydectes knew that the moment had come. This was what he could use to get rid of Perseus once and for all. He told Perseus to bring him back the head of Medusa, a woman who had once been beautiful but who had been raped by Poseidon in the temple of Athena. As punishment for desecrating her temple, Athena turned Medusa into a snake-haired creature so hideous that anyone who looked upon her face would instantly be turned into stone. After her transformation, Medusa was sent to live on an island in the Ethiopian Sea with the other Gorgons, who were the daughters of the Titans Ceto and Phorcys.

Before Perseus set out on his journey, Athena appeared to him, telling him he would first need to visit the Hesperides. They were the nymphs who lived at the very western edge of the world, tending a fantastic garden that held a tree that bore golden apples, which had been a wedding present from Hera to Zeus. Athena told Perseus the Hesperides would be able to help him defeat Medusa.

But first Perseus had to find the way to that divine garden, so he went in search of the Graeae, The Grey Ones. The Grey Ones were sisters of the Gorgons, three hideous old women who had but one eye they shared by passing it from one to the other. Perseus came to the cave of the Graeae. He watched the women passing the eye back and forth, taking turns using it to see. Perseus hid in a dark corner, and when the eye was being passed from one old hag to the next, he jumped out and snatched it away. The Graeae wailed and screamed at Perseus, but he held firm: they would get their eye back if they took him to the garden of the Hesperides. Finally, the women realized they had to do as Perseus asked, so they took him to the garden, and when they arrived there, Perseus gave them back their eye, as he had promised.

Perseus received many gifts to help him on his quest. From the Hesperides, he received a bag to put Medusa's head into. Zeus gave him a sword made of adamant. Hades gave him a cap that would make him invisible. Swift Hermes gave him winged sandals so he could fly, and a polished shield was Athena's gift.

Soon enough, Perseus arrived on the Gorgons' island. All about him were things that looked like statues, but really were the stone bodies of heroes who had tried to kill Medusa and failed. Because it was safe to look at Medusa's reflection, Perseus used the shiny inside of his shield as a mirror to guide him as he walked carefully towards the Gorgons' cave. Using the shield, he looked inside and saw Medusa and her sisters were sleeping. Like a flash, Perseus ran inside the cave. He took his sword of adamant and chopped off Medusa's head. The hair of snakes still writhing, Perseus stuffed the head into his bag. From the bleeding neck of the dead Gorgon leaped Pegasus, a great, winged horse, and Chrysaor, a beautiful young man. Pegasus and Chrysaor were the children of Medusa by Poseidon, and they were born when Perseus killed their mother. When the Gorgons realized Medusa was dead, they tried to chase Perseus, but because he was wearing the magical hat Hades had given him, they could not see him and thus could not catch him.

Perseus next headed towards Ethiopia, where King Cepheus and Queen Cassiopeia ruled. Now, Cassiopeia and Cepheus had a daughter of surpassing beauty, whose name was Andromeda. Cassiopeia boasted that Andromeda was more beautiful even than the most beautiful of the Nereids, the nymphs of the sea. This boast angered Poseidon, for his wife, Amphitrite, was herself a Nereid. Poseidon therefore commanded a great flood and sent a huge sea serpent to ravage the land all about. Cepheus went to the Oracle of Ammon to find out what to do. The oracle said that the floods would stop, and the monster would go away for good if Cepheus and Cassiopeia offered it their daughter. Cepheus and Cassiopeia were horrified by this, but the oracle had no further advice for them. Sacrificing Andromeda was the only way. Cepheus and Cassiopeia therefore took Andromeda and chained her to a rock next to the seashore. With many tears, they bid their beautiful daughter goodbye and then left her to her fate.

Flying with his winged sandals, Perseus approached the coast of Ethiopia, where he saw beautiful Andromeda chained to the rock. Perseus alighted next to her and asked what was wrong. Andromeda explained she was there as a sacrifice to Poseidon, that he might stop flooding the land and sending his monster to eat the people and their livestock. Perseus looked on Andromeda and felt pity for her and loved her. He told her he would help save the Ethiopians from the monster and save her too. He instructed her that once the monster appeared, she must keep her eyes closed and not look at any cost. Andromeda promised to do as he asked.

Perseus hid behind the rock and waited. Soon enough, the sea began to roil, and the waves began to rise: the monster was coming. But Perseus held fast. He waited until the monster was almost close enough to snatch Andromeda in its jaws, and then using his winged sandals he flew in between the princess and the beast. He plunged his hand into his special bag and drew out the head of Medusa. Being careful not to look at it himself, Perseus showed it to the sea serpent. The serpent, being only a beast, did not have Perseus' wisdom, and so looked directly at the head. Even though Medusa was dead, her ugliness was still such that whatever looked at her turned to stone, and the sea monster was no different. The beast shuddered once and then fell into the water with a mighty splash. It sank to the bottom, a dead lump of monster-shaped stone.

Perseus freed Andromeda from her chains and brought her back to her baffled and exultant parents. Andromeda explained what Perseus had done, and the king and queen offered him Andromeda's hand in marriage. Perseus gladly accepted, and soon he and the princess were wed. Perseus and Andromeda returned to his birthplace in Argos as man and wife.

But Perseus had one last task to complete before he could settle in Argos. He returned to Seriphus to see his mother, where he found that Polydectes had continued to pursue her. Perseus vowed that Polydectes would molest Danae no more, so he went into the throne room and said, "Behold, Polydectes, here is the gift I promised!"

Perseus then took the head of Medusa out of the bag and showed it to Polydectes, who immediately turned into stone. As thanks for sheltering himself and his mother, Perseus made Dictys the king of Seriphus. Once this task was done, Perseus headed back home to Argos.

Acrisius learned that Perseus was on his way home. Acrisius was still worried about the prophecy that Danae's son would kill him, so he left Argos and went into exile in Thessaly. But this didn't save poor, greedy Acrisius. He decided to attend the funeral games that the king of Thessaly was holding after the death of his father. Unbeknownst to Acrisius, Perseus was among the competitors at throwing the discus. When it was Perseus' turn, he gave the discus a mighty throw, but it went astray and veered into the crowd where it struck Acrisius on the head, killing him instantly. Thus, the prophecy was fulfilled.

Although Perseus was now heir to the throne, he didn't want to become king by having killed Acrisius, so he gave the throne of Argos to Megapenthes, the son of Acrisius' brother Proetus. In exchange, Megapenthes gave Perseus the throne of Tiryns. Megapenthes also renounced any right to take revenge on Perseus for the death of his uncle.

When all his deeds were done and his throne secured, Perseus returned all the magical items he had received from the gods, with many thanks to their owners. The head of Medusa he gave as a special gift to Athena, who took it and fixed it into the aegis of Zeus, which she carried from time to time.

Perseus and Andromeda ruled wisely and well for the rest of their days, and when they died, Athena set them as constellations in the heavens next to Cepheus and Cassiopeia, and next to the great Pegasus, the winged horse of the gods.

The aegis of Zeus was often described in ancient times as a kind of shawl or wrap. Many representations of Athena show her wearing this, with the head of Medusa prominently displayed on it. Today, we still use the phrase "under the aegis" to indicate protection or legitimacy, because Zeus' aegis was a symbol of his royal power, which Athena might then wield as his proxy when she wore the aegis.

Heracles

Alcmene was a human woman married to a man called Amphitryon. While Amphitryon was away at war, Zeus looked upon Alcmene and wished to make love to her. Zeus took on the form of Amphitryon and went to Alcmene, who did not realize this was a god and not her husband. Alcmene became pregnant by Zeus.

Later that same night Amphitryon did come home from the war for real, and he also wanted to make love to his dear wife, whom he hadn't seen for a very long time. Alcmene welcomed him, and by Amphitryon, she also became pregnant, the same night that she conceived a child by the god Zeus.

Now, Hera, the Queen of the Gods, knew Zeus had been unfaithful to her with Alcmene, and she was jealous of the child. Thinking to cause both the child and Zeus disgrace, when Alcmene went into labor she made a deal with Zeus that the first child born to the House of Perseus would become High King over the Greeks. Zeus agreed, and Hera contrived to delay the birth of Alcmene's twins while hastening the birth of Eurystheus, son of Sthenelus, who did become king when he was a man.

Alcmene gave her son by Zeus the name Heracles, perhaps thinking that by doing Hera this honor she would be appeased. The other twin was called Iphicles, whose son Iolaus became the great Heracles' charioteer.

But Alcmene suspected that naming the baby after Hera would not be enough to pacify the jealous goddess, so she exposed Heracles out on a hillside, to show that she did not want Zeus' child. Kind, grey-eyed Athena saw the baby, though, and saw this was her half-brother, who was destined to become a great hero. Athena, protectress of heroes, picked up the infant and brought him to Hera, who did not recognize him. Hera cooed over the infant, and played with him, and nursed him with milk from her breast, but Heracles sucked too hard, and it hurt her. Hera pushed the baby away, and a spray of milk came out of her breast. The milk went far into the heavens and became what we now call the Milky Way. But the milk did more than that: it gave Heracles many powers of strength and skill and strategy.

After Hera rejected the baby, Athena brought him back to his parents, who raised him. But Hera wasn't done trying to destroy this child: when Heracles and his brother were but toddlers, she sent poisonous serpents into their beds to bite them and kill them. Iphicles was afraid of the snakes and cried, but Heracles picked them up and strangled them. When his nurse came in to check on the boys, she found Heracles waving the dead snakes about, playing with them as though they were toys.

Amphitryon was astounded by what his adopted son had done. He sent for the blind seer, Tiresias, and asked what the fate of Heracles would be. Tiresias, the great and wise prophet, said Heracles would become a hero who would defeat many monsters.

Thinking to make sure young Heracles had a proper education, Amphitryon hired a tutor named Linus to teach the boy. Now, Linus was a great poet and musician, famed throughout the land for the quality of his songs and verses. But Heracles was not a good student. He didn't care much for either songs or poetry, and one day he got frustrated with Linus hounding him to play the lyre properly. Heracles threw the lyre at Linus' head, striking him dead on the spot. Heracles was charged with murder, but he was acquitted based on the argument he had been defending himself against someone who was attacking him. Deciding it wasn't safe to have Heracles in his household, Amphitryon sent the young man out into the country to help look after his cattle.

Finally, Heracles decided it was time to go out into the world to seek his own path. But before he set out, he received a bow and arrows from Apollo, a sword from Hermes, armor from Hephaestus, and a robe from Athena, and for himself, he made a great club of wood. Thus armed, Heracles went to the city of Thebes, where he learned the Thebans were being forced to pay a high tribute to Erginus, king of the Minyans every year. Heracles didn't think this was fair, so he waited for the Minyan emissaries to show up to take the tribute home with them. When they arrived, Heracles attacked them. Heracles cut off their ears, noses, and hands, and tied these around the emissaries' necks, then sent them back to their king saying, "Tell Erginus that's all the tribute he is going to get."

Erginus, of course, was furious. He marshaled his army for an attack on Thebes, but Heracles helped the Thebans equip an army of their own, and when battle was joined great Heracles fought against the Minyans. Erginus and the Minyans were defeated, and as a reward, Creon, King of Thebes, gave his daughter Megara to be Heracles' wife.

Megara and Heracles were happily married for a time. Together they had two children, a son, and a daughter. But jealous Hera wasn't done with Heracles yet: she made him go mad, such that he killed both his children and his wife. But the madness wasn't permanent, and when Heracles came to himself, he was distraught. He loved his wife and children and couldn't believe he had killed them with his own hands. Determined to make amends for his crime, he went to the Oracle of Delphi to find out what he could do in penance. The Oracle told him the best thing he could do was to serve his cousin, King Eurystheus at his court in Tiryns. There Heracles was to do ten deeds that Eurystheus would command of him, and if he succeeded in those deeds, he would become immortal. Heracles didn't like the idea of becoming servant to Eurystheus, who had become king in Heracles place because of Hera's trick and who was weak and cowardly, but he also knew it was dangerous to refuse to follow the advice of the Oracle.

When Heracles arrived at Eurystheus' court, vowing to serve him in ten labors, Eurystheus couldn't believe his luck. Now he had a chance to bring this cousin of his down a peg, and maybe even get rid of him for good without having to do the dirty work himself. So Eurystheus thought of the most dangerous tasks possible and started giving them to Heracles.

The First Labor: The Nemean Lion

The first task was to vanquish the Nemean Lion. The Lion had been terrorizing the country around by kidnapping young women, and then when warriors came to rescue them, killing and eating the warriors. No one had been able to defeat the Lion because its hide was impenetrable. No ordinary mortal sword or arrow could pierce it, and the Lion's claws were so sharp and hard it could tear through even the hardest armor.

Heracles arrived in Nemea and went in search of the Lion. Soon enough, he spotted it, and the Lion saw him. The Lion stalked closer and closer, and Heracles, not knowing weapons could not pierce the beast's skin, fired arrows at it. The arrows bounced off the beast's hide, and still, it came towards Heracles. Heracles took up his club and began to swing it at the Lion. This didn't kill the Lion, but the beast didn't like it much and ran into a cave to hide. The cave had two mouths: Heracles blocked one and went into the other in search of the Lion.

Heracles entered the cave silently. He hefted his club, ready for the Lion's attack. Suddenly, the Lion shot out of the darkness straight towards Heracles. Heracles gave his club a mighty swing at the Lion's head, stunning it. Heracles dropped his weapons and ran over to the groggy beast. He grabbed it around the neck and squeezed with all his might until the Lion was dead.

As Heracles stood over the body of the dead Lion, he thought, "That hide can turn away any kind of weapon. I bet it would make the best armor."

So, he took out his knife and tried to skin the Lion but try as he might he couldn't pierce the animal's magical hide. Heracles was frustrated and about to give up, when grey-eyed Athena appeared to him and said, "Use one of the creature's own claws to skin it."

Heracles thanked the goddess and did as she suggested, and in no time, he had skinned the Lion, keeping the hide in one piece. The head of the Lion Heracles put on his head as a helmet, with the golden mane falling about his shoulders, and he used the skin of the forelegs to tie it about his neck, with the fearsome claws still attached at the ends.

Having completed the first task, Heracles marched back to Eurystheus' court, proudly wearing the lionskin. He strode into the throne room, saying, "See, Cousin? I have completed the first task. I wear the skin of the Nemean Lion."

But cowardly Eurystheus was so frightened by the lionskin he jumped into a nearby urn and ordered Heracles never to bring the evidence of his conquests into the city again, but rather to display them outside the walls. He also ordered Heracles not to come into the court precincts anymore: instead, he was to wait outside the city and Eurystheus would give him his next instructions there.

The Second Labor: The Lernean Hydra

The second task Eurystheus set Heracles was to slay the Lernean Hydra. The Hydra was a terrifying monster, the daughter of Typhon and Echidna, a swamp-dweller with nine heads, one of which was immortal, whose breath and blood was poisonous, and whom jealous Hera had raised specially to kill Heracles. Accompanied by his nephew, Iolaus, Heracles set out for the swamp, covering his mouth and nose with a cloth to protect himself from the Hydra's fumes.

Heracles and Iolaus arrived at the Hydra's lair, where Heracles fired a flaming arrow into the water. When the Hydra rose up out of the swamp to face this threat, Heracles struck at it with his mighty sword, slicing off one of its heads. Except in the place of the head that had just fallen, two more sprang up. Heracles tried again, but the same thing happened.

Heracles called out to his nephew for help. Iolaus thought quickly and then ran to kindle fire. He took a flaming torch in his hand and said, "Uncle, slice off the creature's heads, and I will seal the wounds with the torch."

Working together, Heracles and Iolaus attacked one head after another, Heracles slicing it off with his mighty sword and Iolaus plunging the torch into the wound so another head couldn't grow back in its place. But as they were getting ready to fight the last, immortal head, Hera saw they were winning and sent a huge crab to distract Heracles. The crab nipped at Heracles' heels with its claws, but the great hero paid it no mind: he stomped on the crab and crushed it, then went about chopping off the remaining, immortal head, and the Hydra was dead. Heracles took the remaining, immortal head, which was still alive and moving, and placed it under a huge rock. He also dipped his arrow points into the creature's poisonous blood. Hera, meanwhile, upset that the hero had killed two of her pets, took the Hydra and the crab and placed them in the heavens as the constellations Hydra and Cancer.

Heracles and Iolaus went back to Eurystheus in triumph. Disappointed that Heracles had been successful and, worse still, was still alive, Eurystheus warned that tasks would only get harder from here. He also said that killing the Hydra wouldn't count towards his ten tasks, since Iolaus had helped slay the creature.

The Third Labor: The Ceryneian Hind

The next thing the wretched king demanded Heracles do was to capture the Ceryneian Hind, a golden-antlered deer so fast that it could outrun an arrow. Now, the Hind itself wasn't dangerous like the Lion or the Hydra had been, but it was an animal sacred to Artemis, goddess of the hunt. Eurystheus was hoping that if Heracles caught it, that Artemis would punish him, and that would finally be the end of the hero.

Heracles set out on the hunt for the Hind. He looked up and down and here and there, and finally one morning as he was awaking he saw a flash across the meadow. It was the shine of the Hind's golden antlers. Swift Heracles ran towards the Hind, but even he wasn't fast enough to catch it. He chased the animal all through Greece; he ran after it all through Thrace; the Hind eluded him through Istria and the land of the Hyperboreans. Heracles pursued the Hind for a full year, but never could he get close enough even to touch it.

Finally, the Hind began to tire, and it lay down to sleep. Heracles saw this and wove a soft net. He threw the net over the sleeping Hind, and thus captured it. He put a leash around the Hind's neck and began to lead it back to Eurystheus' court. But Heracles knew this was an animal sacred to Artemis, so as soon as he chanced upon one of her temples, he stopped and prayed to her, explaining why he had the Hind, and that it was part of a penance assigned by the Oracle at Delphi. He promised he would set the animal free as soon as he had shown it to Eurystheus. Artemis appeared to Heracles and listened to his prayer. She agreed to let him show the Hind to the king, as long as he set it free immediately afterward. Heracles thanked the goddess and set out for Tiryns.

When Heracles arrived at Tiryns, he called for Eurystheus to come and see the wonderful Hind. Eurystheus looked down upon the hero and the animal from atop the city walls, then told Heracles, "Bring the animal inside the city and put it in the menagerie with my other beasts."

But Heracles knew he couldn't do that: he had made a promise to swift Artemis that he would let the Hind go. So, he took the leash off the Hind's neck, whereupon it immediately bounded away. Heracles shouted to Eurystheus, "If you want this animal for your zoo, you will have to catch it yourself."

The Fourth Labor: The Erymanthian Boar

Eurystheus was furious that Heracles had let the Hind go, and that he had been so successful in each of the dangerous tasks he had been set. So, he thought and finally decided to send Heracles on an adventure that would be the most dangerous yet: to capture the Erymanthian boar and bring it back to Tiryns, alive. Now, the boar was a fearsome beast, huge, strong, and old, with tusks as long and as sharp as sabers. No hunter who had encountered it had ever returned from the hunt alive. Eurystheus thought that surely this task would be the end of the great hero.

Heracles put on his lionskin cloak and took up his weapons, and headed for Mount Erymanthos, a place that was home to many wild beasts, including the boar. On the way, he stopped to visit the centaur Pholus, who was an old friend of his. Pholus offered the hero dinner, and when Heracles asked for wine Pholus at first refused. He only had one jar, and it had been a gift from Dionysus himself. What was more, if he opened it, the smell would attract other centaurs. Heracles convinced Pholus to open it anyway, and sure enough, all the centaurs from the neighborhood round showed up asking for a drink. But they forgot to water down the wine, and soon they were all quite drunk.

Now, a drunk centaur is a nasty centaur, and they soon started attacking Heracles. Heracles didn't want to hurt Pholus' friends, but he had no choice. He shot at them with his arrows he had dipped in the blood of the Hydra. The ones that he hit dropped dead on the spot; the others ran away toward the cave of Chiron, the greatest of the centaurs.

As Heracles was firing at the retreating centaurs, one of the arrows accidentally hit Chiron, who hadn't been at the party and who hadn't been attacking Heracles. Heracles was devastated at this. He pulled out the arrow and put on some medicine that Chiron told him to use, but it was no use. Some say Chiron soon died of the wound; others say that he was immortal, but the pain from the poison was so great that he offered up his immortality in exchange for Prometheus' freedom, and that Heracles set the Fire-Bringer free after this.

Pholus was curious as to how Heracles had been able to kill the others so quickly, so he picked up an arrow. He wasn't careful with it, though, and ended up pricking his skin with it, poisoning himself as well.

Once Heracles managed to get free of the rampaging centaurs, he continued his hunt for the boar. He found the animal on a mountainside, but it eluded him. Heracles chased it for some days but couldn't subdue it until he was finally able to drive it into a deep bank of snow. The boar became stuck in the snow, and Heracles was able to throw a net over it and capture it. Heracles put the great boar on his mighty shoulders and marched back to Tiryns in triumph. When he arrived, he shouted for Eurystheus to come and see his catch. Eurystheus came to the city walls, where he took one look at the boar. The beast was so terrifying to him that cowardly Eurystheus ran away and hid.

The Fifth Labor: The Augean Stables

King Augeas was a ruler wealthy in cattle. He had so many animals it was impossible to keep the stables clean. Eurystheus thought that maybe he could defeat the great Heracles not by pitting him against monsters, but by making him clean up mountains of dung, a humiliating task for a mighty warrior.

Heracles went to Elis, where Augeas was king. Without mentioning that he was there at Eurystheus' bidding, Heracles told the king, "I can cleanse your stables in one day if you will pay me a portion of your herds."

Augeas was surprised that anyone would offer to clean the stables at all, never mind boast they could do it in a single day, so he accepted Heracles' offer. Heracles then had all the animals moved out to pasture. Then he went and diverted the courses of two rivers, the Alpheus and Peneus so they flowed down and through the cattle-sheds, sweeping away all the dung in one powerful surge. When the sheds were clean, Heracles put the rivers back into their beds.

Augeas was astounded. But when he learned that Heracles had done this at Eurystheus' command as part of his penance, he refused to pay. Augeas agreed to submit to arbitration over the dispute, but when his son Phyleus came forth saying that Augeas had indeed made a deal with Heracles to pay him, Augeas forced Heracles and Phyleus to leave the country. Heracles eventually went to war with Augeas to exact payment. After defeating Augeas' army and killing the king and sacking the city, Heracles put honest Phyleus on the throne. In gratitude for his victory, Heracles competed in Olympian games at Elis and founded twelve altars to the immortal gods there.

Heracles returned to Tiryns to let Eurystheus know the task had been completed. But word had come to Eurystheus that Heracles had demanded payment for it, and so Eurystheus said that cleansing the stables would not count among the ten tasks Heracles was required to perform.

The Sixth Labor: The Stymphalian Birds

On the shores of Lake Stymphalis was a large wood in which a great flock of birds had made their nests. Now, these were no ordinary birds: if any human walked near or through those woods, the birds would set upon them and eat them alive. The people who lived near the lake were in constant fear of these flesh-eating birds. Eurystheus decided that ridding the country of those birds would be the next task for the great Heracles.

Heracles arrived at Lake Stymphalis. He wasn't worried about being set upon by the birds himself since there was no way they could pierce his lion-skin armor. But he was puzzled about how to get rid of so many creatures. As Heracles sat and thought, grey-eyed Athena appeared to him. She gave him a rattle of bronze made by skilled Hephaestus, and this was the very thing Heracles needed.

Heracles used the rattle to make a thunderous racket that startled the birds from their trees. As soon as the birds took flight, Heracles put down the rattle, then took up his bow and shot the birds from the sky. Heracles went all the way around the wood, putting up the birds and then bringing them down, one by one. Soon all the birds were dead, and the people of the lake were free from their terror.

The Seventh Labor: The Cretan Bull

Asterius, king of Crete, had died without an heir, and Minos wished to ascend the throne. To convince the people of his right to be king, Minos said he had the favor of the gods and that they would give him whatever he prayed for. So, Minos made sacrifice to Poseidon and prayed for a great Bull to come up out of the sea, promising that if Poseidon answered his prayer, he would then immediately sacrifice the animal. Poseidon heard Minos and sent a great Bull of surpassing size and beauty out of the sea. The people of Crete then agreed that Minos had the favor of the gods and made him their king. But Minos did not keep his promise to Poseidon: The Bull was too beautiful to sacrifice, he thought, and so he put it amongst his herds and sacrificed another in its stead.

This angered Poseidon greatly. He therefore cursed Pasiphae, Minos' wife and queen of Crete, with an unquenchable lust for the Bull. She went to Daedalus, the clever builder, and told him to make a hollow statue in the shape of a cow, one the Bull of Poseidon could not possibly resist. Daedalus did the queen's bidding, and she hid within the Bull. Soon enough, the Bull came and mated with what he thought was a fine cow, but really it was Pasiphae inside the statue he was coupling with. Soon Pasiphae found herself pregnant by the Bull. The son she bore had the head of a bull and the body of a man, and it was called the Minotaur. Minos imprisoned it in the labyrinth, which was also built by Daedalus, where it lived until it was killed by the hero Theseus, whose tale shall be told later.

Eurystheus decided that sending Heracles to capture the Cretan Bull would be his next command, for Poseidon had made the animal untamable as part of his revenge for Minos not making it into a sacrifice. Heracles arrived at Crete and explained to King Minos what he wanted. Minos said he was welcome to take the Bull, but that Heracles would have to capture it himself; neither Minos nor any of his men would help with that task because the Bull was too dangerous.

Heracles soon captured the Bull and brought it back to show Eurystheus. The beast was too fearsome for the king's menagerie, so Heracles let it go loose. It roamed through Sparta and Arcadia until it came to Marathon, where it laid waste to the countryside until the hero Theseus killed it.

The Eighth Labor: The Mares of Diomedes

The Mares of Diomedes were a gift to King Diomedes from the war god, Ares, and were ferocious horses so savage they refused to eat grass and grain as their common cousins did. Instead, they had been taught to eat human flesh. Word of these horses came to Eurystheus. If monsters and man-eating lions had not been enough to bring down the great hero, perhaps flesh-eating horses would do the trick. Eurystheus therefore told Heracles to go and bring back the Mares of Diomedes.

Heracles went to the stables where the horses were kept. There he attacked Diomedes and fed him to his horses. Once they had devoured their master, the horses became docile and never again desired to eat flesh. Heracles brought the horses back to Tiryns, where Eurystheus dedicated the horses to the great goddess Hera.

The Ninth Labor: The Belt of Hippolyta

Word of Heracles' successes had spread throughout all of Tiryns. Everyone followed his exploits and waited for news of what new deed he would perform. The royal family was no exception to this, and one day Eurystheus' daughter came to her father and said, "Please, father, may I set the next task? Have mighty Heracles fetch the belt of Hippolyta, queen of the Amazons, for I wish to have it for my own."

Eurystheus granted his daughter's request and told Heracles that he must bring back the belt of Hippolyta.

Heracles went to the city of Themiscyra, on the banks of the Thermidon River, where the Amazons lived. The Amazons were a race of women warriors, trained in battle, who cut off their right breasts so they would be unhindered when using their weapons. Their left breasts they kept so they could nurse their infants. So skilled and courageous were these warriors that they were beloved of Ares. Hippolyta, their queen, was far and away above the others in her prowess, such that Ares had given her a belt as a token of his esteem, and it was this belt that Heracles had been sent to fetch.

Heracles went before Hippolyta and explained his errand. Hippolyta ignored him, and instead sent her Amazons to fight with Heracles. The Amazons were strong and swift, and cunning with their weapons, but Heracles was mightier still, and soon he had defeated them all. Last he fought with Queen Hippolyta. It was a ferocious battle, but in the end, Heracles killed the powerful queen and took her belt, which he brought back to Eurystheus.

The Tenth Labor: The Cattle of Geryon

The tenth deed Eurystheus commanded Heracles to do was to bring back the cattle of Geryon. These were fine, beautiful cattle, whose coats turned red when touched by the light of the sun. Now, a herd of cattle might not seem to be such a terrifying foe, but it wasn't the animals who were the dangerous part of this task. No, indeed, to get to the cattle, first Heracles would have to get past the cowherd,

Eurytion, and his two-headed dog, Orthus. These might not seem so daunting, either, after Heracles' adventures with the Hydra and the Nemean Lion. But Geryon himself was not to be trifled with. The son of Chrysaor, he who had sprung from the neck of Medusa, and of the Oceanid Callirhoe, Geryon was a three-bodied giant who had four wings. He was a vicious warrior, terrifically strong, and ferociously guarded his cattle.

Geryon and his herds lived on the island of Erytheia, a far place in the most distant reaches of Oceanus, the encircling sea. The first problem Heracles had to solve was how to get there. Heracles walked across the breadth of Europe and coming to the end of the Iberian Peninsula he set up two pillars, one at the tip of Iberia and another across the straits in Libya, as markers of his journey, on which he had many other adventures not told here. The sun was hot in Iberia, so much so that Heracles was feeling angry about it, so he nocked an arrow to his bowstring and pointed it at the sun in his irritation. Helios, the Sun god, was so surprised and amused by Heracles' presumption that he loaned the hero a boat that would take him to Erytheia.

When Heracles arrived on Erytheia, he first slew Eurytion and Orthus. Then he had a long and difficult battle with Geryon, who had the advantage of six arms and three heads, not to mention he was a giant and much bigger than Heracles. But soon Heracles defeated Geryon too. He loaded the cattle into the boat the Sun had lent him, and sailed back first to Tartessus, where he returned the boat to Helios. After this, Heracles drove the cattle back to Tiryns, completing his tenth deed at the command of King Eurystheus.

The Eleventh Labor: The Golden Apples of the Hesperides

Now, Heracles had worked for King Eurystheus for eight years and one month and had completed the ten deeds the oracle had demanded, but Eurystheus still wasn't satisfied, and he refused to let Heracles leave his service. Eurystheus declared that killing the Lernean Hydra and cleansing the Augean Stables hadn't counted, because in the first instance Heracles had help, and in the second he had demanded payment. So Eurystheus told Heracles he had to perform two additional deeds, the first of which was to fetch golden apples from the garden of the Hesperides.

The tree that grew the golden apples had been a wedding gift from mighty Zeus to Hera. This tree she put in a garden at the end of the world, and it was guarded by a great dragon, and by the Hesperides, nymphs who were the daughters of the great Titan, Atlas. Their garden was at the very end of the world, and no hero had ever been able to get past the dragon to take the apples.

Some say that Heracles made his way to the garden and killed the dragon with arrows dipped in the poisonous blood of the Hydra, but others say he obtained the apples using a trick he had learned from Prometheus, and this is how that came about. The garden of the Hesperides was at the edge of the world, near where the Titan Atlas held up the sky. Heracles knew the Hesperides likely would allow Atlas to take some apples since he was their father. So, Heracles strode up to Atlas and said,

"I would like some apples from the tree in your daughters' garden, and in exchange, I will hold up the sky for you while you are away."

Atlas agreed and shifted the burden of the sky onto great Heracles' shoulders. It was a heavy burden to bear. Heracles soon felt that he could not hold it up for much longer. But then the Titan Atlas reappeared, carrying three apples. Atlas looked at Heracles and said, "I think you are doing a fine job of holding up the sky. There's really no need for me to take it back."

Heracles nearly panicked. He did not want to be stuck holding up the sky forever. But then he thought of a way to trick Atlas into taking the sky back. Heracles said, "I can keep holding the sky for you, but it's cutting into my shoulders. Can you take it back for a while so that I can find some padding?"

Atlas agreed to take the sky back on his shoulders, whereupon Heracles snatched up the apples that the Titan had placed on the ground and left the garden of the Hesperides, never to return. And poor Atlas still stands under the weight of the sky, which he cannot put down.

The Twelfth Labor: Cerberus, Dog of the Underworld

Heracles returned to Tiryns bearing the golden apples. Upon his return King Eurystheus set him one final task, thinking that maybe this would be the one that would finish off the great hero. Eurystheus told Heracles that he had to bring back Cerberus, the three-headed dog who guarded the gates to the Underworld.

Heracles marched into the Underworld and went before Hades. He asked the dreaded god whether he might borrow Cerberus because this was the final task he had to perform to satisfy the oracle and leave the service of Eurystheus. Hades agreed on one condition: Heracles had to subdue the dog without using any weapons.

Now, Cerberus not only had three heads: he also had a serpent for a tail. Heracles therefore would have to protect himself from sharp teeth at not one, but two ends of the giant animal. Covering himself in the thick hide of the Nemean Lion, Heracles went in search of Cerberus. The hero found the great hound at the gates of Acheron, one of the five rivers that flowed through the Underworld. Mindful of his agreement with Hades, Heracles approached Cerberus empty-handed. He leaped upon the great dog and put his arms around its throat. Cerberus struck at mighty Heracles with its serpent's tail, but the serpent could not bite through the lionskin. Heracles squeezed and squeezed, and soon Cerberus was cowed by the chokehold.

Heracles returned to Tiryns, the great hound at his heels. He showed the dreadful creature to King Eurystheus, who declared Heracles' penance done, and released him from his service. And as he promised, Heracles brought Cerberus back to Hades.

The great Heracles had many other adventures that have not been told here. Heracles fought with monsters, helped on quests, and did many heroic deeds before he died and was placed among the stars by the eternal gods.

Theseus and the Minotaur

Aegeus was king of Athens, and his friend Pittheus was king of Troezen. Aegeus had no heir to his throne, so he consulted the Delphic Oracle about what to do. The oracle said something confusing: it seemed to indicate that Aegeus shouldn't drink any wine until he got to Athens. Wanting to make sure he understood the oracle, he went to Troezen for advice. Aegeus told Pittheus what the prophecy was. Pittheus understood it and told Aegeus he should not make love to a woman until he returned home to Athens. Pittheus had a daughter named Aethra, and he convinced Aegeus to take her back to Athens with him and take her into his bed when he got home.

Soon enough, Aethra became pregnant by Aegeus and gave birth to a son whom she called Theseus. Aegeus decided he would set a task for the child to do when he had grown into a man, a task that would prove him worthy to be king of Athens when Aegeus was gone. So, Aegeus buried a sword and a pair of sandals beneath a great rock. He told only Aethra that he had done this so that only Theseus would know where to look.

Theseus grew into a young man, tall and strong, and skilled with all kinds of weapons. His mother told him about the rock with the sword and sandals underneath it. Theseus decided the time had come for him to seek his fortune in the world and to take up his inheritance, so he went to the rock and, putting his mighty shoulder to it, pushed it aside. He took up the sandals and the sword and set out for Athens. Theseus had many great adventures on his way to Athens.

When Theseus arrived at Athens, he found that the sorceress Medea had become consort to King Aegeus, his father, and had been trying to help him get more children. Medea realized who Theseus was, but Aegeus did not. Medea feared Theseus and convinced Aegeus he was an enemy. Medea told Aegeus to invite Theseus to a banquet and there give him a cup of poison in place of wine. Aegeus agreed to this.

Theseus went to the banquet as Aegeus' guest, and the cup of poison was put before him, but Theseus did not drink of it just then. When the meat was passed at the table, Theseus drew the sword that he had taken from beneath the rock, as though he were going to use it to cut some meat for himself. Aegeus saw him do this and, recognizing the sword, grabbed the cup of poison and dumped it out, and welcomed Theseus into his household as his son and heir.

Making Theseus heir to the throne of Athens did not sit well with the sons of Pallas, who also dwelled in Athens and who had thought the throne should be theirs when Aegeus died. The sons of Pallas, therefore, went to war against Aegeus, and they set up an ambush against Theseus and his men. But a herald of the Pallantides saw this and told Theseus what was waiting up ahead. Theseus and his men, therefore, were ready when the ambush came, and they defeated the Pallantides, who were all killed or scattered.

Theseus went back to Athens with a will to making himself useful and beloved of the people. The very first thing he did was to deal with the Cretan Bull that Heracles had loosed on the countryside. The people were grateful to Theseus: The Bull had been destroying their fields and orchards, and no one had been able to kill it or make it go away. Mighty Theseus captured the Bull and sacrificed it to the eternal gods.

Besides the Cretan Bull, the Athenians had one other very great sorrow. Many years ago, Androgeus, son of Minos, king of Crete, had come to Athens to participate in athletic contests. But Androgeus never went home again: some say he went out to try his luck against the Cretan Bull and was killed by it; others say that Aegeus feared he might support the Pallantides against him and so assassinated him. Whatever the cause of Androgeus' death, Minos went to Athens to demand satisfaction, but Aegeus would not hear him. Therefore, Minos declared war on the Athenians, and since his cause was just the gods sided with Minos and brought drought and famine along with the destruction of war.

In desperation, the Athenians prayed to Zeus and asked what they could do to end their suffering. Zeus told them to give Minos whatever he asked of them. Minos demanded that every nine years Athens should send a tribute of seven youths and seven maidens to Crete. The Athenians agreed, and this brought an end to the war, drought, and famine. But the tribute was the beginning of another kind of suffering. Minos took those young people and locked them in the Labyrinth, a winding, confusing maze of tunnels and walls in which dwelt the Minotaur, half-man, half-bull, who feasted on the flesh of those who lost themselves within his maze. The agreement with the Athenians said that Minos could do this as long as the Minotaur should live.

Soon after Theseus arrived in Athens, it came time for the tribute of young people to be sent to Crete once more. Theseus arranged it so he would be among the youths of the tribute, for he thought he might be able to kill the Minotaur and thus bring an end to the tribute once and for all. The young people were supposed to be unarmed, but Theseus managed to hide a sword in his clothing. In token of the mourning of the people of Athens for the young men and women who were being sent to their awful fate, the Athenian ship sailed out to Crete with black sails. Aegeus hoped Theseus would make good his promise and come back alive, and he wanted to know as soon as possible what the outcome of his adventure had been. He made an agreement with the ship's captain that when the ship returned to Athens, it should have white sails if all was well, or black sails if Theseus had failed and was dead.

The ship set sail for Crete. When it arrived, Minos and the royal household and the people of the city came to see the new tribute that had been sent to feed the Minotaur. Ariadne, the daughter of Minos, looked upon Theseus and, seeing that he was an unusually handsome young man, fell in love with him. Ariadne determined to help Theseus and so went to him bearing a ball of thread. Ariadne told Theseus to affix the thread to the gate of the Labyrinth and to unspool it as he walked through the maze. To find his way out, Theseus had only to follow the clew back to the entrance.

Theseus thanked Ariadne. He bid the other young people wait for him near the entrance of the Labyrinth, then did as Ariadne instructed, reeling out the thread as he proceeded through the maze. After what seemed like days, Theseus came to the center of the Labyrinth. There stood the Minotaur, a huge beast with massive horns. Only the head was that of a bull; the rest of the body was that of a man, thick and muscular. The Minotaur charged at Theseus, and there was a fierce battle. In the end, Theseus was the victor, and the Minotaur lay dead.

Following the thread, he had spooled out, Theseus returned to the entrance of the Labyrinth. Gathering up the young people, he shepherded them back to the harbor. Ariadne had also been waiting outside the Labyrinth, anxious to see whether Theseus would survive. She asked Theseus to take her with him, and he agreed. Some say that Theseus and his friends escaped by putting holes in all the Cretan ships so they could not follow him, but, however it came about, the Athenians could escape without being harried by the Cretans.

It was a long journey back to Athens. One night, the young people stopped on the island of Naxos to rest. While they were sleeping, the god Dionysus came and looked upon Ariadne. He fell in love with her and carried her away to be his bride. When Theseus and the others awoke in the morning, they saw that Ariadne was gone. They called and searched for her, but she was nowhere to be found. With heavy hearts, they got back on board their ship and set sail for Athens.

Between the rush to escape from Minos and their grief at the disappearance of Ariadne, the Athenians forgot to change the sails on their ship. Now, Aegeus had stood on the Acropolis every day since Theseus' departure, keeping a lookout for the return of his son, and when he spied the returning ship and its black sails, he cast himself down from the rock in despair, thinking that Theseus was dead, and so perished.

Theseus arrived at a city in confusion. Some were in mourning over the death of Aegeus, others were rejoicing at the return of Theseus and were eager to crown him king. But before taking the throne, Theseus made sure that the proper sacrifices and rituals were performed for Aegeus. And when he finally did become king, Theseus made many wise laws and helped to strengthen the city in many ways.

The image of the Labyrinth and the Minotaur had a lasting effect on European culture, extending even to medieval Christian sacred architecture. Craig Wright notes that the labyrinths that decorate the floors of many French cathedrals once held the image not of Christ or other Christian symbol but of the Minotaur. Wright says the Minotaur likely was a symbol for the Devil and that the progress into and out of the cathedral labyrinth was meant to symbolize Christ going into Hell to free the souls there between his crucifixion and resurrection.

Part 2: Roman Mythology

A Captivating Guide to Roman Gods, Goddesses, and Mythological Creatures

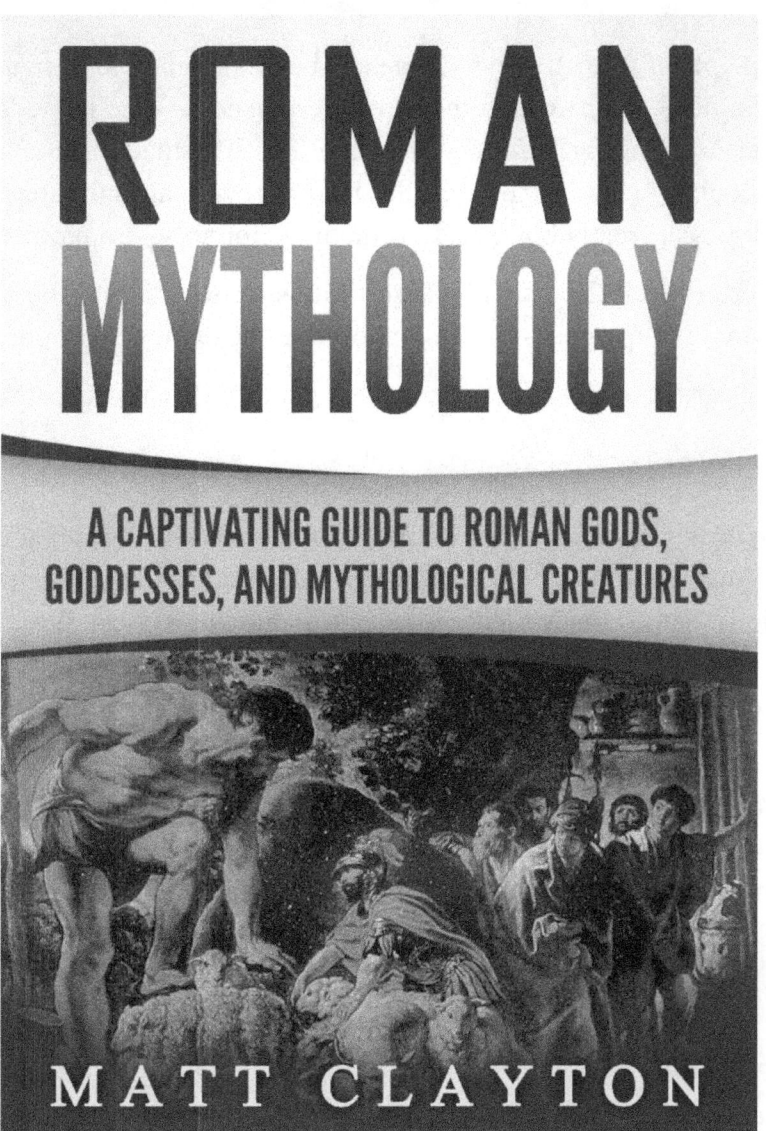

Introduction

Gravitas was a founding principle of Roman society. Life can be brutal, and the Romans figured out early that guiding one's actions with weightiness or seriousness—or, in today's word—intentionality—was necessary. Using *gravitas* as a guide for life made them exceptionally practical—although not particularly creative. In fact, the Romans were an unimaginative society. The creativity they did employ was greatly borrowed –sometimes forcibly--from other cultures.

Only a few of their gods were entirely Roman. Because little is written during the early years of Rome, it is difficult to separate their own divinities as opposed to those they appropriated.

Originally, the Romans were farmers. Many of their earliest gods dealt with crops, rain, and their main river—the Tiber.

Gravitas, with its intentionality and practicality, led the Romans to think affinities could be cultivated by making their gods look like those of their neighbors. These affinities made assimilation or conquest much easier. Allowing citizens to keep their religious traditions, a widespread practice among some early civilizations, helped make them more compliant with Roman rule. And if Roman traditions looked like the traditions of the conquered peoples, the subjugated populace would believe they truly belonged to Rome.

Like a modern exercise in building a commercial brand, Roman writers of the first century BC developed stories of Roman myth and history to manufacture legitimacy for their rulers. Virgil (70–19 BC), for instance, gave Rome its most important work of authority—the *Aeneid*, which told the story of Rome's roots in the Trojan War; they were descended from Trojans, the enemies of the Greeks. We'll take a brief look at the truth of this possibility in "Chapter 4 — Borrowings from Etruria."

The Shape of Things to Come

We will look at many aspects of the Roman gods, goddesses, and mythological creatures. Each of the first six chapters begins with a narrative scene which helps bring the legendary and mythical characters to life.

In chapter 1, we explore the seeds of legitimacy that Virgil planted regarding the Trojan connection to Rome. Though Aeneas was a minor character in Homer's epic *Iliad,* Virgil shows Aeneas to be the epitome of what a good Roman should be—heroic, serious, virtuous, and devoted. And, important to the *Iliad*, Aeneas was one of the sons of Venus or, as she was known to the Greeks, Aphrodite—the goddess of love.

How do we get from a Trojan demigod to the reality of Rome? This is the topic of chapter 2. In this chapter, we explore the foundation of that great city by the semi-divine, wolf-suckled brothers, Romulus and Remus. We also consider the myth of Aeneas's son, Ascanius, who was also known as Iulus—the basis of the name of Julius, and the basis of the Julio-Claudian dynasty of the Roman Empire. Virgil gave the family of Julius Caesar its back-story to make his patron, and Rome's first emperor, Augustus, seem worthier of being a living god.

In chapter 3, we examine the gods of Roman origin as well as Roman mythological creatures.

Chapter 4 focuses on the Etruscan influence on Roman mythology. Latin culture co-opted Minerva as its own, and then gave her the Greek attributes of the goddess Athena.

Perhaps the strongest influence in Roman mythology came from the Greeks. The Greeks were far more creative, and their legends were far richer and more detailed. The Greek influence is the topic of chapter 5. The Greeks had expanded their influence to the southern portion of the Italian peninsula far from the tiny Kingdom of Rome. In the centuries before the Roman Republic, the Greeks had expanded into southern France and eastern Spain.

In chapter 6, we delve into the world of Celtic influence and see how the gods of the Celts were melded with the Roman pantheon in creative ways. What we know about the Celtic pantheon comes from the Romans. The Celts used oral storytelling to record their history for generations.

Finally, in chapter 7, we take a brief look at the potential truths behind the Roman gods, goddesses, and creatures. Every myth had a beginning, and in this chapter, we explore some of the possibilities.

The Romans were builders and innovators in many industries. They took existing resources and shaped them to suit their needs. But they also adopted the creative ideas of others. Over time, the Roman pantheon became increasingly a melting pot of ideas blended into a cultural potpourri.

Chapter 1 — The Trojan Connection

Goddess Juno—Jupiter's queen—looked down upon the ragtag fleet of Trojan ships, led by Aeneas, and she sneered with delight as she thought of sinking them to the bottom of the sea. Juno despised Troy and its people. Petty and immature, like all the gods and goddesses—they lacked the maturity and humility to act wisely.

She hated Troy because of Paris, Prince of Troy, snubbed Juno when he judged who was the most beautiful goddess—between Juno (the Greek Hera), Minerva (Athena) and Venus (Aphrodite).

The dispute began at the wedding of the Greek goddess, Thetis, to King Peleus of Aegina.

One goddess, though, despised the event. Eris, goddess of discord, and daughter of Jupiter and Juno was not being invited because the other gods wanted a peaceful event. Her exclusion angered her. She said, "to the fairest one" and threw a golden apple over the wall and into the party. No one caught the apple, but three goddesses claimed the golden apple as her own—Juno, Minerva, and Venus. To settle the dispute, they asked Jupiter to judge between them.

Understanding the potentially dire consequences of such a task, Jupiter chose a mortal to judge who should own the apple based on the inscription: "to the fairest one." That mortal was the fair-minded Paris, Prince of Troy. Jupiter understandably protected himself by choosing Paris, since the choice would upset the two goddesses not selected—and that hostility might last forever. Jupiter protected his own sanity and safety by transferring the dangerous duty onto an expendable and convenient mortal. Perhaps even wise Minerva did not realize how truly foolish Paris would be to accept such an inherently dangerous task.

After the wedding celebration was over Mercury (Hermes) escorted the three goddesses to Asia Minor—also known as Anatolia, or modern Turkey. There, they bathed in a local spring on Mount Ida, not very far from Troy. After freshening up, they found Paris, sitting on a log under the shade of a mature tree, tending to his flock on the slopes of the mountain. Naturally, the prince was surprised to have the three lovely goddesses present him with this interesting challenge.

At first, the goddesses posed before the honest prince--Juno, Minerva and finally Venus. But Paris could not decide.

"I'm afraid, my ladies," he said, taking a deep breath before continuing, "that this is an impossible task. You are each incredibly beautiful, and my mind is at an impasse."

"What if we were to show you our full form," asked Venus, "without the visual impediment of the divine clothing we typically wear out of sensible modesty?"

The other two goddesses nodded encouragingly.

Paris smiled. He had seen naked women before and knew the pleasure that came with the sight. In fact, his wife was the beautiful mountain nymph, Oenone. The thought that three major goddesses would willingly bare themselves for his judgment aroused him more than he thought possible.

He spoke cautiously, though. He knew of their power, and he did not want to answer rashly and risk offending any of them.

"I can sense the importance of this challenge you've given me. If it pleases each of you that I—a mere mortal—view your beauty in its entirety to complete the charge you've laid upon me, then I will humbly do this thing as you request. I sincerely hope that this will be enough to settle in my own mind an answer to your question."

Again, Juno went first because of her seniority amongst the three goddesses. Quietly, she unfastened her garment and let it fall to her feet. Slowly, she stepped out of it and moved toward the young man as he remained seated.

Closer she came, slowly advancing. When she was close enough to touch, she showed the young man her neck and breasts down to her abdomen. She showed him her thighs and buttocks, as well as the small of her back. As she displayed her physical form in all its splendor, she whispered to him, bribing him in exchange for his vote for her. She would give him rule over all of Europe and Asia, and not merely Asia Minor—from Eriu to Yamato—Ireland to Japan.

As Juno returned to her clothes, the other two goddesses guessed what she had done. Each secretly decided to sway the young prince's decision with the best possible bribe they could consider.

Next, Minerva dropped her clothing and approached Paris, equally seductively. Because of her temperament as a warrior and protectress of the homeland, her movements added power and finesse which Juno lacked. Her earthiness left Paris breathless. As Minerva displayed up-close each curve of her beautiful body, she whispered to him that she could make the young prince the wisest and most skilled of all mortals in the art of war. All he would need to do was to choose her as the owner of the golden apple.

Moments later, as Minerva restored her vestments, Venus dropped her gown and stepped forward, turning with a coy seduction that left the young mortal's heart pounding with each step. This was the goddess of love and Paris felt once again the impossibility of this challenge.

Venus promised that if Paris chose her, she would make it possible for him to marry the most beautiful mortal woman in all the world—the already married, Helen, wife of King Menelaus of Sparta.

Assailed by so much feminine charm, the bribe which raked most heavily across his mind was the one that most closely matched the feelings overpowering his mind, body, and soul. Helplessly, he chose Venus and thus sealed the fate of Troy, setting in motion events that would eventually lead to the creation of Rome.

When Helen left her husband to join Paris in Troy, the Greeks banded together to attack the Trojan capital. Why would there be such unity amongst the usually conflicting Greek city-states? The leaders of those city-states had agreed to that attack.

Helen was so beautiful that almost every king in the Greek kingdoms sought her hand in marriage. Her wise father feared any man he chose for his daughter would soon lose her because the others would continue to fight over her, even after she married. Minerva's wisdom guided him to bind each king to the father's decision by swearing to protect Helen's marriage to whomever she was to be pledged. Only after each king gave his pledge did the father reveal his choice.

Thus, when Helen left her husband, the other Greek kings were duty-bound to go after her—to protect her marriage to Menelaus of Sparta. For a decade, they laid siege to Troy to protect those wedding vows between Menelaus and Helen. In the end, Troy lost, and the city was destroyed.

Now that Juno and Minerva had ensured the collapse of Troy, after its ten-year war against the Greeks, its remaining citizens were dispersed throughout the eastern Mediterranean. The future heritage of Troy depended upon Aeneas, second cousin of the now dead princes of Troy—including Hector, Paris, Deiphobus, Polydorus.

Juno despised Troy for several reasons.

From her great height, Juno also looked down upon her favorite city—Carthage—and dreaded the thought the descendants of Aeneas would someday ruin the now-fledgling town. If only she could stop Aeneas and end the prophecy concerning him.

Juno also despised the Trojans because her own daughter, Hebe, had been replaced as Jupiter's cupbearer. Her husband had chosen instead the Trojan, Catamitus (Greek Ganymede).

After the destruction of Troy, Aeneas had directed his ships to head west. Somewhere out there was a new home for him and his people.

Slowly, at first, and then with conviction, Juno descended down to Earth and to the island of Aeolus—master of the winds.

"My dear King Aeolus," said Juno.

"My goddess!" Aeolus stood back, amazed at her sudden entrance. "To what do I owe this honor."

Juno looked away for a moment, considering her words carefully, then turned back to him with a look that drilled into his eyes, commanding his full attention, even though she already had it. "I have come to ask a favor. A tiny thing, really. It's trivial, but it needs to be done."

"Yes, my lady?"

"I would like you to use your winds to create a storm. Over there," she pointed out to sea, "are the ships of Aeneas, the Trojan prince, and all his fellow refugees. I want them destroyed—especially the ship holding Aeneas."

"Hmm-mm," Aeolus nodded thoughtfully, then shook his head in disagreement. "My lady, I cannot. I have no grievance with Aeneas or his people."

"But you must," said Juno. "Perhaps I could make the task more attractive by including Deiopea to become your bride."

The king's eyebrows raised in appreciation of the offer. The sea nymph, Deiopea, was said to be the loveliest of all sea creatures. But he shook his head again. "My lady, I will not take her as wife, for I already have one, and she is sufficient for me. But because this means so much to you, I will help."

"Thank you, kind sir," said Juno, and abruptly vanished.

Immediately, Aeolus gathered all his winds and overwhelmed the Trojan fleet. This storm disturbed the surface of the sea, and suddenly, Neptune (Greek Poseidon) was alerted to the commotion in his realm.

"What goes on here?" Neptune demanded. He saw the winds and their target—the Trojan ships. The sea god had no love for Troy, but he resented the intrusion into his domain. "Be still, waters!" he commanded. And he calmed the winds, despite the efforts of Aeolus. This was Neptune's territory, and any intrusion by another god was unwelcome.

Neptune could smell the handiwork of Aeolus and knew someone else was behind this attack. Despite his dislike of the Trojans, he disliked the intrusion even more. So, he gave the ships of Aeneas a favorable breeze which took them to the north coast of Africa, not far from the new town of Carthage.

Aeneas and his fellow travelers landed on the shore, thankful to be alive.

In the distance, Aeneas saw a beautiful woman approaching on horseback. She had a bow strung across her shoulder and a quiver on her back. He watched her as she made her way to them.

"You are all lucky to be alive," said the woman, who happened to be his mother, Venus, in disguise. "Some of the gods favor you and your companions."

"I was beginning to lose hope," said Aeneas. "I appreciate your words, but even I was beginning to wonder if all of the gods might be against us, now that we have lost our war with the Greeks."

"Fear not," she said, "your destiny is to plant the seed of a great empire."

The young prince cocked his head to the side, uncertain he could believe this from some strange huntress on the beach of North Africa.

"And you are in luck," she said. "Not far this way," she pointed toward the West, "there is a new town called Carthage, founded by the Phoenicians of Tyre, and ruled over by good queen Dido. You will usually find her in the Temple of Juno."

"Well, thank you, fair stranger," said Aeneas, just as she prodded her horse into a trot in the same direction. "But—" and she was gone, receding into the distance, ignoring his words.

"I see trees over there, master," said one of his fellow travelers. "There may be a well and clean water."

"Good. Let's us refresh ourselves and then head toward this new town, Carthage."

Aeneas found his way to the Temple of Juno and there entreated the queen to help his small band of refugees. In the tradition of all civilized folk, she invited him and his fellow travelers to a banquet in their honor.

In the meantime, Venus met with her son, Cupid—half-brother to Aeneas.

"My darling son, I need your help. I would like you to help me create a bond between Queen Dido and your brother, Aeneas."

"Yes, mother."

At the banquet which Dido arranged for Aeneas and the other Trojans, Cupid showed up disguised as Ascanius, Aeneas's son by his first wife, Creusa. While the image of the son approached Queen Dido bearing gifts, invisible Venus surrounded the real Ascanius with a ghostly shroud to keep others from noticing there were two of him. Even the real Ascanius was bewitched into ignoring the imposter.

Dido graciously received the gifts and reached for the handsome young boy to draw him close. She felt an overpowering urge to give him a mother's affection. While in Dido's embrace, Cupid worked his charms on her, weakening a sacred pledge she had made to stay faithful to her dead husband, slain by her brother.

"Tell me, Aeneas," said Queen Dido, "all that has happened to you. I want to hear the entire story. Stories help us to understand." She was going to say that stories also entertain, but thought better of it, knowing the Trojan's tale would include great tragedy.

"Well, my lady," said Aeneas, "I would like to thank you for your gracious hospitality. We are weary from our travels. This spot of civilization soothes our souls."

The queen raised her cup toward him and smiled.

"Our once-great city," said Aeneas, "at the entrance to that enormous body of water, northeast of the Mediterranean—what the Greeks call the Euxine Sea—our city was attacked by the Greeks. For ten long years, they tried to destroy us all. Then, on the eve of what seemed like our victory, the Greeks left a gift on our doorstep and departed en masse. But the gift was our undoing, for within it was Greek soldiers who lay as still as death until we were drunk and asleep from our long celebration.

"By the end of the next day, our city was a smoldering mass of former humanity. Our people killed or under Greek subjugation. Some of us escaped inland. The next day, when the hostilities were done, and some semblance of peace returned, I went back to Troy to find my wife, but she was dead. In the smoke, I saw an image of her, and it spoke, telling me I would establish a great city to the West.

"Inspired by her words, I convinced my fellows to help me build our small fleet of ships. Our travels took us all over the Eastern Mediterranean—to Thrace, where we found the remains of our fellow Trojan, Polydorus. Then to Strophades, where we met Celaeno, the Harpy. She told us to leave her island. And before we left, she said I must look for a place called Italy. After that, we landed at Crete. We thought perhaps we arrived at our destination and began to build our city. We named it Pergamea. But then Apollo visited us and told us we had not yet arrived at our true destination.

"At fair Buthrotum, north of Macedonia, we attempted to replicate Troy. On that island, we met the widow of Prince Hector and found Prince Helenus who had also escaped. Now, Helenus has the gift of prophecy. From him, I learned more about my own destiny. He told me I needed to find Italy which is also known as Ausonia, and by the name Hesperia."

"There are two large peninsulas named Hesperia," said the queen. "One is due north of here, across the Tyrrhenian Sea. The other is at the far western end of the Mediterranean, north of the exit to our small, inland sea, and entrance to a far larger, Great Ocean, the realm of Atlas and the once great Atlantis which sank so long ago."

The queen suddenly felt self-conscious about what she had just said. The Phoenician custom was to keep secret the discoveries of the Phoenician people. Such discoveries were frequently made at great cost and to give them away would be to lose the Phoenician hold on such knowledge. But the queen had been feeling exceptionally joyous with the arrival of these guests. She felt overcome with a generous spirit.

"Thank you, my lady, for your help in our quest. After Buthrotum, we found ourselves in a land called Trinacria where our ships barely escaped a grave danger we later learned was called Charybdis—a vast whirlpool which threatened to swallow entire ships. From there, we encountered the Cyclopes and one of the Greeks—a soldier who had served under Ulysses—a soldier who had been left behind in their mad rush to escape the great, one-eyed beasts. We took Achaemenides, the Greek, on board with us, but barely escaped with our own lives when blind Polyphemus heard our voices. Not long afterward, my own father, Anchises, died peacefully of his own years. We sailed next into the open seas, unsure where to find this Hesperia—this Italy. A great storm nearly destroyed us, but then we found the coast not far from here."

"I am so thankful that you made it," said the queen. Her eyes glistened toward him, and at that moment, she knew she loved this prince.

Aeneas, too, could feel the bond and gazed upon her with deep admiration.

Later, after they had taken in their fill. Dido suggested Aeneas, and a few of his best hunters go inland with her to find game.

In the hall, but invisible to these mortals, Juno confronted Venus.

"Listen," said Juno. "I would like to strike a bargain with you. These two seem to be well-suited for one another. See how much they are in love?"

"Yes," said Venus, "what did you have in mind."

"I will stop my attacks on these Trojans if Aeneas stays here in Carthage with Dido, becoming her husband."

Venus smiled at the thought of her son marrying the local queen. This pleased her greatly. And since she already orchestrated the beginnings of love, she would do everything she could to hold Juno to her promise.

During their hunt, Dido and Aeneas followed their clues to find their prey and became separated from the others. And when a storm struck they found a nearby cave for shelter. Within the cave, Aeneas held Dido close to keep her warm. In that embrace, there came kisses and a deeper, more passionate experience which Dido took to mean Aeneas was now bound to her for life.

After they returned to the palace in Carthage, the two were clearly and deeply in love. But their affection was short-lived. While the two were together in her chamber, a bright light appeared in the middle of the room and suddenly there appeared the form of Mercury, messenger of the gods.

"Aeneas, son of Venus," said Mercury, "this has gone too far, and Jupiter himself has commanded me to intervene. You have a destiny, and it must be seen through to the end."

"But," said Dido. "does he have to stay away. Can't he return to me?"

"I'm afraid not, my lady," replied Mercury. "The future fate of the world hangs on the shoulders of Aeneas."

Dido shook her head and screamed in agony. The pain of such fresh love being snuffed out before its full blossom was too much to bear. She looked to Aeneas for some relief from her agony.

"Sorry, my love," was all he could say.

Her screams filled the palace with such remorse all could feel her pain.

Immediately, she grabbed the sword of Aeneas and left the room.

Cautiously, he followed. He could hear her commands to build a pyre in the great opening in front of the palace. When it had been built, she climbed up to the top of it, his sword in her hand.

"People of Carthage. We've all suffered too much tragedy of late. First, the murder of my husband, and now this tragic love that must never be. Suddenly, she plunged the sword into her abdomen.

Her eyes goggled in incredible pain, and she dropped to her knees, the sword sliding from her wound. "There will forever be great strife between our peoples, Aeneas. You have wounded me more than this sword could ever do." She then fell backward onto the pyre, gasping these final words, "rise up from my bones, avenging spirit."

Understanding the gravity of this act, Aeneas quickly gathered his people and ushered them out of the city and back to their ships.

As they sailed away, he looked back at Carthage, but all he could see was the smoke pouring upward into the sky from Dido's funeral pyre.

What History and an Analysis of Myth Tell Us

Estimates for the founding of Carthage range from 1215 to 814 BC. Modern historians seem to favor the later date, because of a reference made by Timaeus of Taormina that Carthage had been founded 38 years before the first Olympiad (776 BC). This is ironic and possibly quite wrong, if we believe the story of Aeneas, because the Trojan War was supposedly far earlier—traditionally dated at 1184 BC. Some historians placed the founding of Gadir (Roman Gādēs, Moorish Qādis, modern Cádiz, Spain) at about 1104 BC, as a colony of Tyre—far beyond Carthage when traveling from Tyre. While it's entirely possible that Tyre bypassed many locations to establish a lonely outpost beyond the far, opposite end of the Mediterranean, it seems more likely they created at least one or two intermediate colonies across that 4,000-kilometer length. The archaeological level at Hissarlik, Turkey, associated with the Trojan War, called Troy VII was destroyed about 1220 BC.

Though Aeneas has minor mention in Homer's *Iliad* the myth of Aeneas being the grandfather of Rome came about during the first century with writers like Virgil, Ovid, and Livy. So, it seems highly probable the Roman connection to Troy, was contrived to establish a pseudo-historical basis for the Julian family brand.

From this fictionalized narrative, Julius Caesar could claim direct descent from the goddess Venus, through her son, the Trojan Aeneas. In addition, Aeneas's father, Anchises, was fourth grandson of Zeus and Electra. Thus, every time a member of the Caesar family spoke, they were speaking from a position of divine power, and this helped them to command greater respect. It didn't save Julius Caesar from the conspiracy to assassinate him, but it did help to lay the foundation of "gravitas" that grew into the office of emperor.

Venus was the goddess of love, but Julius Caesar had made a name for himself, and his extended family, more from his own acts of war—against the Celtic Gauls, and later against disruptive elements within the Roman Republic.

From these histories (contrived or handed down), we learn which gods favored the Romans and their founders.

Some of the other gods were no friend to Rome and its founding. These defacto enemies of Troy, and thus, by implication, of Rome, were Juno (Greek Hera), Vulcan (Hephaestus), Mercury (Hermes), Neptune (Poseidon), Thetis (no counterpart in Roman mythology), Timorus (Phobos), Formido (Deimos) and Discordia (Eris). Discordia (Eris), after all, was the goddess who had started the entire Trojan problem with her jealous spitefulness for not being invited to a divine wedding. It seems doubly abusive she should be against the party being attacked because of her own behavior. Supporting Troy, and by inference, also Rome, were Venus (Aphrodite), Apollo, Mars (Ares), Diana (Artemis), Latona (Leto) and Greek Scamander (no Roman equivalent).

From the expanded story of Aeneas, by the Romans, we see Jupiter also supported the Roman cause.

From Aeneas, the son of Venus down to the founders of Rome—Romulus and Remus—there were 15 generations of Latins, first at Lavinium and then at Alba Longa.

In the next chapter, we see how these divine, Trojan demigods struggled to establish a beachhead in the middle of the Italian peninsula, amongst numerous other tribes.

Chapter 2 — Founding of Rome

"Numitor is the rightful king," said someone in the crowd.

"Then why did he make it so easy for his brother, Amulius, to depose him?" asked Domitianus, "Does it sound right that such a reckless and weak king should remain on the throne? Numitor is too soft."

"If I steal your cloak," asked Remus, "does that make me the new owner?"

"If you were weak enough with your protection of your own property to permit its theft, then, yes," said Domitianus, "you would no longer deserve it." Remus did not miss the fact that his opponent had shifted the focus from Domitianus to Remus, apparently incapable of considering himself ever to be vulnerable.

"And," Remus raised a small purse of coins, "this used to be on your person, but you could not feel it when I took it? Does that make you weak and soft?"

"Give that back," said Domitianus reaching out for it.

"Why?" asked Remus. "It's mine, now. You said so in your own words."

Domitianus clenched his fists, furrowing his brow, and worked his mouth as if chewing a tough slab of beef. He stepped toward Remus, but one of his friends held him to keep him from taking another.

"Remus has a point," said Romulus. "Amulius stole the throne by force—betrayal from within. If I were Numitor, I'd have Amulius drawn and hanged by his own entrails for his betrayal. Simple treason. You don't do that to your own king. Betrayal is one of the worst of crimes."

Remus continued to taunt Domitianus by dangling the coin purse in front of him. Suddenly, Remus attempted an underhanded toss which was poorly aimed—not with conscious intent—and hit Domitianus in the face with his own purse.

Enraged, Domitianus attacked Remus and the violence quickly spread throughout the crowd.

Romulus called for his supporters to withdraw. "Retreat, my friends. These traitors are not worth our time."

So, they departed, fending off the last few blows from their opposition.

When Romulus and his friends had retreated to a safe distance, they noticed the supporters of King Amulius also retreating, carrying their wounded.

"Where's Remus?" asked Romulus. He looked from one friend to another. They shrugged. "By the gods! They've taken my brother!"

"What do we do?" asked someone nearby.

"We rescue him," replied Romulus, sharply.

"Yes, yes. Of course," said another. "But how?"

"Iulianus, follow them," said Romulus. "Find out where they're holding my brother and report back."

The young man—their fastest runner—nodded and took off after the supporters of the usurper. Romulus spent the next hour gathering men to support a rescue effort. Not long afterward, Iulianus reported back and gave the location where Remus was being held.

Minutes later, three groups of Numitor's supporters approached the holding place by different paths and quickly overwhelmed the guards standing outside. Two others had been taken with Remus and all three of them were freed.

That evening, both Romulus and Remus received word King Amulius was looking for them. This was followed shortly by a message which took them both by surprise. It was from Numitor himself. He wanted to meet the two young men.

It was late in the evening when Romulus and Remus were led to the home of Numitor, the deposed king.

"Welcome, lads. Please," he motioned toward seats in front of a table toward the center of the room. "I have enquired about your family. Faustulus informs me that he found you both being suckled by a woman of the Rasennan wolf clan, not far north of here. She gave you two up to him, for she had merely found you both drifting on a raft on the River Tiber."

"Yes," replied Romulus. "That is as much as we know."

Numitor nodded. "I heard how you stood up for me against the supporters of my brother." He smiled.

"I am surprised," said Romulus, "that your brother would let you live after taking your throne."

"Yes," said Numitor, smiled weakly and turned from them, continuing to speak. "He has my daughter, Rhea Silvia, in a convent which they control. After Amulius led his forces to overthrow me, he had my son killed, and had my daughter committed to 30 years of celibacy in the convent to ensure I could not have an heir." Numitor nodded and turned back to them. "My brother fears me, but cannot kill me. It's ironic he can kill babies, though. He killed his nephew easily enough. But perhaps he feels it's safer to keep me alive so my supporters don't kill him outright."

"If only there were something we could do," said Remus.

"Perhaps there is," said the former king. "Perhaps there is. But first, let me tell you a story. Do you know of Aeneas?"

"Yes, of course," said Romulus. "Every child of our tribe learns of the great Trojan, descended from the gods—from Venus directly, as her son, and from Jupiter through his father, the fifth great-grandson of Jupiter, himself."

"Many of us," said Numitor, "are directly related to Aeneas and to the gods. When my daughter was locked away in the convent, Mars visited her."

"Really?" asked Remus. "In a convent?"

"He is a god," said Romulus.

"And my lovely Rhea has divinity running through her veins, just as it does through those of my brother. But she gave birth to twins." Numitor paused for a moment, looking deeply in the eyes of Remus, and then Romulus. "Amulius ordered those twins to be killed, but the servants put them in a basket and set them adrift on the River Tiber."

Romulus's eyes went wide, and he looked at Remus, who was equally surprised. "But—"

"When Aeneas reached these shores," continued Numitor, "he made friends with King Latinus of the Latins. The king was so impressed by the Trojan that he offered him his daughter, Lavinia, in marriage. This did not sit well with King Turnus of the Rutuli, for he had expected Lavinia's hand in marriage. Turnus therefore attacked, but Aeneas prevailed and killed Turnus. Aeneas founded the city of Lavinium, named in honor of his new wife.

"After the death of Aeneas, his son, Ascanius—also known as Iulus—became the king of Lavinium. A greedy Etruscan king, named Mezentius, attacked after Ascanius's installation as king, forcing the people of Aeneas to pay tribute. Not long afterward, Ascanius attacked Mezentius, killing his son, and forced the Etruscan to pay tribute. When that had been settled, Ascanius left the city under rule of his step-mother, Lavinia, and he went on to found this city of Alba Longa."

"But wait," said Romulus, "What was that you said earlier about twins and the river?"

Numitor smiled and nodded. "I am the twelfth great-grandson of Aeneas and you, my two wonderful boys, are the fourteenth great grandsons of Aeneas."

Both young men stood and again looked at one another. Numitor stepped toward them and flung his arms around them both, drawing them close for a strong embrace. "You are my grandchildren," he said. "I knew it the moment I heard of your strength of character, your support of me. You have the blood of the gods running in your veins." He stopped and wept, holding them tightly. They both embraced their grandfather.

Through the night, they talked about how to restore Numitor to the throne. Within three days, they had gathered the necessary forces and developed the strategy to overthrow Amulius, while also protecting their mother, Rhea Silvia. In the fighting, Amulius was killed along with many of his supporters. Those who were left were told to submit to Numitor or to face exile.

Both boys wished their grandfather well, but felt their destiny lay back where the Etruscan wolf woman had nurtured them. They returned to the seven hills of their upbringing vowing to build an even greater city. With their grandfather's blessings, they returned to the home they knew.

"There," said Romulus, "on the Palatine Hill. That is the most strategically defensible position for a new city."

"I disagree," said Remus. He pointed, "There, on the Aventine Hill."

They argued for several minutes, finally deciding to let the gods help in their decision.

"Let augury help us," recommended Remus.

"Agreed," replied Romulus. "Begin!"

"There, there, there," said Remus excitedly. "I have spotted six auspicious birds.

Romulus grumbled and waved for his brother to be patient. A few moments later, he said, "Well, now. Look at that. Twelve. I win."

"But I spotted mine first," said Remus. "I win."

Romulus shook his head and muttered, "Incredible. Do what you must. I'm building my city there." Again, he pointed to the Palatine Hill and waved to his followers. "Let's go."

Remus looked back to those who remained with him. "To the Aventine Hill," he said. "Perhaps we'll have two cities in support of each other."

Before long, Romulus and his men had built a wall partway around their new city. Remus decided to investigate the defenses and leaped over the wall. A surprised guard whirled on him and thrust his sword into the young man before the guard recognized who it was.

"By the gods," remarked Romulus, "what have you done?" He rushed forward and held his brother in his arms. "Remus, oh Remus!" The life went out of him and Romulus wailed with grief.

For several days, his men, combined with those who had followed Remus, continued to build the wall. Romulus, however, stood apart from them, working through his grief.

Finally, he gathered his men together to talk with them.

"This city has one major problem."

"But sir," said one of his men, "what could that be. The site is good," he looked to some of the men who had followed Remus, "perhaps as good as the Aventine Hill, and our wall is sturdy and highly defensible. What are we missing?"

Romulus chuckled and then smiled for the first time in over a week. "As we are now, we are a city of only one generation. After we are gone, so will be our city."

"What?"

"Oh," said one of the others. "Of course. No women."

Suddenly, everyone laughed.

"What I propose," said Romulus, "is that we negotiate with the Sabines just beyond these hills and ask for their daughters in marriage."

Everyone nodded. It sounded like a good plan, but when the Sabine elders were consulted, their answer was a resounding "No!" Those elders feared the competition. A new city-state in their midst could only mean eventual tyranny, overthrow, or conquest.

Though his men were disheartened, Romulus, smiled a sly grin as he gathered them once again to discuss their options.

"Men," said Romulus, "we have great skills—building, metallurgy, farming and the like. We, therefore, should be able to come up with a plan to gain the women we need. I propose that we prepare a feast and invite our neighbors to join us. Let us finish our wall, and use that as a guise for the celebration. We need weapons, but we also need food. We need to plan this carefully so that it is both enticing to our neighbors and foolproof in our aims to gain our future wives. In a few weeks, about the time we will be finishing our wall, there is the festival of Neptune Equester—god of the sea as patron of horses. We should have some horses by then, too."

Everyone nodded. And Romulus set them each to the tasks in preparation for their upcoming festival.

On the day of the feast, people from all the neighboring villages came—Sabines, Caeninenses, Crustumini, and Antemnates—bringing their sons and daughters to help the new Romulans consecrate their new city and to celebrate the completion of the outer wall.

Midway through the festivities, Romulus gave the signal and half his men grabbed a woman and took her forcefully back up to the wall. There, some of the men remained to guard their catch and keep them from escaping, while others used their new weapons to fend off the angry fathers and brothers. Then, more of the men grabbed another batch of young women to take to their wall, so all would have wives.

Only a small force was needed to guard the women. Most of Romulus' forces were employed to defeat the neighboring men and their wives, forcing them to retreat.

After the guests left, the kidnapped women were taken, one by one, to see Romulus. He talked to each of them, pleading with them to submit to their new husbands for the sake of their new civilization. He appealed to their maternal instincts, suggesting there is nothing more sacred than to share in the creation of children.

The next day, the King of the Caeninenses brought his army and attacked the Romulans. Their king was killed and their army was sent home, demoralized by their humiliating defeat.

Romulus gathered his strongest troops and attacked their city, Caenina, and easily took it. On the first of March, 752 BC, Romulus celebrated the defeat of the Caeninenses by dedicating ground for a temple to Jupiter.

The Antemnates attacked Romulus's new city. And again, Romulus retaliated, capturing their city. Then the Crustumini took up arms against the forces of Romulus and they, too, lost their town.

Finally, the Sabines decided Romulus needed to be vanquished for his theft of their women. King Titus Tatius sent his forces against the gates of the new city and found that one of the women would open the gates if she would receive what they wore on their arms. She was Tarpeia, daughter of Spurius Tarpeius. When she opened the gates, she was immediately killed by their advancing shields—borne on their arms--squeezing the life out of her. Her dead body was thrown off a nearby high rock which came to be known as the Tarpeian Rock—the place Rome executed all traitors.

Now, the Sabines held the city's citadel. The Romulans attacked but were easily repulsed. Romulus's men were depressed by their failure to reacquire their own city.

Romulus talked to them, attempting to lift their spirits. "By Jupiter himself, we will win this. And in his honor, I will build another temple, this time to Jupiter Stator. The gods are on our side if only we will do the brave thing and take these invaders down."

With his men sufficiently motivated, they attacked and sent the Sabine general running. As they closed in on their Sabine enemies, Romulus and his men received the shock of their lives.

Suddenly, between the opposing forces, the Sabine wives rushed to stop them.

"Hear me!" said one of the women, "oh men of Sabine and husbands of Romulus. We do not care to lose either our husbands or our fathers. Please, put down your arms, or you will have to use them against us. We cannot live without fathers or husbands. Please do not make us choose."

The war ended abruptly. King Titus Tatius agreed to rule with Romulus over both the new city and the old city of Sabinium.

As the final agreements had been made, one of Romulus' men spoke, "Sir, we have called this place our city or the city of Romulus, but we truly need a name worthy of a city. Perhaps we could call it simply, 'Romulus.'"

King Romulus looked down for a moment in all humility and then addressed first the man and then all his men. "My fellow countrymen. I am honored by this suggestion, but I would not want to forget my dear brother, Remus. Perhaps we can use his name, instead."

"Or," said another man, "we could use a shorter name that would remind us of both brothers—Roma."

Several others nodded or voiced approval of the new name.

"Yes," said Romulus. "This name makes me happy. I'm sure Remus would approve."

From the She-Wolf to the Founding of a Great City

The first time the story of Romulus and Remus appeared in Roman literature was toward the end of the third century BC. Whether their story had always been a part of the Roman culture is unknown. Many cultures had oral traditions that were eventually written down for posterity—the Greeks, the Germans, and the Romans.

Romulus and Remus were suckled by a she-wolf. The image seems to shout, "We are tough; don't mess with us." Modern scholars consider the wolf symbol to have been Etruscan (Rasennan). What might be more likely, if these two legendary heroes are based on real people, is they were suckled by an Etruscan maiden (human). Etruria (Rasenna), at the founding of Rome, included much of the surrounding terrain, with its capital at Velzna, northwest of Rome.

Many other cultures occupied what is today modern Italy. Modern-day Tuscany was home to the Etruscans, and in southern Italy and Sicily, Greeks occupied many places along the coast.

The tiny kingdom of Rome had a great deal of competition on the peninsula, including the two main islands associated with Italy: Sardinia and Sicily.

The city of Lavinium is, a real place, and archaeological evidence suggests Alba Longa was a real town or group of smaller towns along Lake Albano, stretching from the Alban Mount.

It took a great deal of practical, as well as military wisdom for the Romans to survive and to thrive amongst so many other cultures.

But the Romans had the gods on their side. Roman humility to the higher power of the gods made those mortals modest enough to seek practical and workable answers, instead of relying on their own, shortsighted egos.

Chapter 3 — Purely Roman Gods

Around 640 BC, King Ancus Marcius led his people down to the Tiber in a slow, solemn procession.

Ancus Marcius Rex, King of Roma, at age 37, had only recently become the tiny kingdom's new ruler. His predecessor was the grandson of Hostus Hostilius, the hero who fought alongside Romulus in reclaiming the city from the Sabines. Hostus died a hero, and his grandson made a fine king but paid too little attention to worship of the gods. Ancus was a Sabine by lineage, and grandson of the city's second king—Numa Pompilius—the great successor of Romulus.

As his first act, he ordered the Pontifex Maximus to make a public copy of the text of his grandfather's commentaries on religious rites, so every citizen knew the details of proper worship.

His people were soon intent on appeasing the god of the river—Tiberinus.

Four men carried a straw effigy of a man on their shoulders. They walked up to the edge of the water and waited.

"Citizens," said the king, "Let us first invoke Janus, the god of beginnings to bless this event so that everything we do here will have a righteous impact on our lives. Lord Janus, visit us now and consecrate these proceedings as only you can." He turned from one side to the other to survey the crowd, including them all in what he said.

"We gather today," the king continued, "to pay homage to Tiberinus and to his waters which bring life to the land. Please accept this offering of ours which symbolically links us to the river which bestows to us so many blessings every day of our existence."

A priest from one of the temples stepped forward and consecrated the straw effigy, saying several words of prayer over it. Then the four men threw the straw man into the river, and everyone watched as the current carried it toward the sea.

"Thank you, my good people," said the king, "and may the festivities begin."

There was a loud cheer from the crowd, and everyone walked back up the hill to where the eating and games were held.

Ennius Cloelius was an old man with white hair, but he walked erect despite his age. As counselor to the king, he was frequently found by the king's side. Today was no exception. As they walked behind the crowds of people, they talked.

"My Lord," said Ennius, "I've received reports that a number of the Latin tribes are becoming jealous of our successes. I fear they may attack."

"Thank you, my friend," replied the king, "It's always good to know the truth of things, even when bad news. We need to be prepared, certainly."

"But, Lord, how do we respond if they do attack?"

"With strength, certainly. We defend ourselves. But more than that, we need to realize the people of each city are not necessarily responsible for the acts of their rulers or their military. I, for one, would welcome more citizens, if they are willing to live in peace. As Romulus had done before us, we need to bring more of the Latins into our midst and give them a home within our protection. If more attack us, we defeat them, too, and take their citizens as booty—not as slaves, mind you, but as honored guests and citizens of our new nation."

"Thank you, my Lord. And how will we be legitimizing our attack on the Latins?"

The king laughed. "You're testing me?" He chuckled again and slapped the advisor on the back with affection. "As always, we consult the gods. We will only ever declare war on others through the rites of the fetials. After all, we do want to win, if we do go to war. The last thing we need is to attack and to find that the gods are against us in that attack. That would be foolish, indeed."

"I see, my Lord. Very wise."

"And, as always, my old friend, I rely on your wisdom to tell me when I need to rethink my case."

Earliest Rome

Rome had a habit of acquiring gods along with their conquest of territory and their peoples. The gods included here are those which inherently part of the Roman culture or were imported in the beginning when they kidnapped their Sabine brides.

Abundantia is the goddess of abundance and prosperity.

Bubona is the goddess of cattle.

Candelifera is the goddess of childbirth. The name literally means "she who bears the candle," perhaps referring to someone who provides light for deliveries made at night.

Carmenta is the goddess of childbirth and prophecy.

Clementia is the goddess of forgiveness and mercy.

Cloacina is the goddess of the sewers in Rome, and protector of sexual intercourse during marriage.

Deverra is the goddess of midwives and women in labor. The name means "to sweep away," and this is aimed at the evil that might threaten the mother or newborn child.

Dis Pater is the Roman god of prosperity derived from the land—minerals, metals, crops and more—and later of the underworld. How did the realm of the dead become associated with crops and minerals? Everything connected with the ground was also connected to the underworld. The dead were buried in the ground. Beyond the ground, as the old myths went, the gods ruled over the dead souls. Later, Dis Pater was absorbed into the god, Pluto, who was the counterpart to the Greek god of the underworld, Hades. Pater comes from the root for "father," and sometimes the god was merely called "Dis."

Edesia is the goddess of food who presided over banquets.

Fabulinus is the god of children and teaching them to speak. When an infant spoke their first word, an offering would be made to this god in thanks for the blessed event.

Felicitas is the goddess of good luck and success. Similar to Fortuna, but the luck coming from Felicitas was always positive.

Fides is the goddess of loyalty, trust, and good faith. Her symbol was the turtle-dove, and she oversaw the protection of all state treaties with foreign countries.

Honos is the god of military honors and chivalry.

Janus is the Roman god of beginnings, endings, and the doors or openings between states, realms, and conditions. We see his name even today in the Western calendar for the year's first month—January. Because everything important has a beginning, Janus was the first god consulted at such events—marriages, births, seasons, days, deaths, and even new buildings, and towns. All religious ceremonies had their beginnings. If a festival of Neptune were being held, Janus would be mentioned first, so the celebration begins on the right footing.

Romans held a fascination for omens. They were forever looking for signs to tell the future, and as the present passed through the doorway into the future, Janus was always present demanding consideration from each righteous Roman citizen. As the god of doors, Janus had some say about who could communicate with the other gods and was always consulted in matters concerning any divinity.

The god Janus likely derived from a conflation of two Etruscan gods—Ana (goddess of beginnings), and Aita (god of endings and the underworld).

Juventas is the goddess of youth, especially for the young men who have come of age and were "new to wearing the toga."

Lares was not the name of an individual god, but the term used for all personal, family gods. These gods looked out for the family, its members, and the spirits of its ancestors. Small offerings were given each day to the Lares so they would continue to take care of their dead ancestors and to look out for the good fortunes of the family. During more important functions, more elaborate offerings were made to the Lares in proportion to the importance of the event, whether it be a wedding, birth or some other occasion. See "Penates" for another group of protective gods. Roman cities had public Penates and Lares to protect them.

Larunda is the goddess of silence. She is famous for both her beauty and talkativeness. She was so loquacious she could never keep a secret. When Jupiter had an affair with a fellow nymph—Janus' wife Juturna—Larunda told Juno all the juicy details. For this betrayal of the King of gods to his wife, Jupiter cut out Larunda's tongue so she could never speak again, and Mercury escorted her to the underworld. Taken with her beauty, Mercury made love with her. To keep his affair with her a secret from Jupiter, Mercury hid her in a woodland cottage where the King of gods would never find her. The children she bore became known as the Lares. See also Muta and Tacita.

Liber and **Libera** are a pair of gods—male and female, who represented fertility. Liber was especially important in this patriarchal society as a symbol of male fertility, as well as the personal transition of a boy into manhood. The worship of Liber also involved partying. He was so popular early Romans dedicated an entire month to the adoration of this god. Celebrations included the symbol of male fertility—a giant phallic emblem which was paraded through the city to protect the current season's crops. Later, Liber was superseded by the Roman equivalent of Greek Dionysis, Bacchus. Liber was held in high esteem by traditionalist cults who desired to perpetuate the wild sex parties and the rare slaying of a partygoer which heightened the sense of pleasure.

Muta is the goddess of silence. Her name means "the mute one." See also Larunda and Tacita.

Ocnus is the Roman god of delay, hesitation, and frustration—everything to do with unsuccessful efforts, and is the son of Tiberinus. He was kept in the underworld, condemned forever to weave a rope made of straw. The rope was eaten by a donkey as fast as he made it, thus symbolizing the futility over which he had been given domain.

Penates, like Lares, was not the name of an individual god, but the term applied to all household gods. While the Lares were protective, ancestral spirits, the Penates were gods of Roman households and guardians of storerooms and hearths. Roman cities had public Penates and Lares to protect them.

Pietas is the goddess of duty, loyalty, filial piety and proper religious behavior.

Pomona is the goddess of fruit trees, fruitful abundance, and orchards. She is a wood nymph.

Quirinus is an early Sabine addition. He is a god of war, long before Roman borrowed Greek Ares and renamed him, Mars. Later, when Mars was the defacto god of war, Quirinus became associated with Romulus, elevating the legendary founder to a form of divinity. Thus, Quirinus later represented Rome itself.

Sancus is the god of loyalty, honesty, and oaths.

Sors is the god of luck, possibly a son of Fortuna (see the chapter on Greek gods).

Spes is the goddess of hope.

Tacita is the goddess of silence. Her name means "the silent one." See also, Muta and Larunda.

Tempestes is the goddess of storms and sudden changes in weather.

Tiberinus is a Roman river god for the River Tiber, which ran through the capital city. Like many primitive societies, the Roman culture was at least partially animistic—viewing the world around them as possessing a dual nature—part physical and part spiritual. Tiberinus is the god who helped Aeneas when the Trojan first arrived in Italy. He suggested which allies should help Aeneas defeat the jealous Turnus who wanted Lavinia's hand in marriage. Tiberinus also rescued Rhea Silvia after her imprisonment in the convent. With a Greek female fortune teller named Manto, he had a son named Ocnus. Each 27 May citizens create a straw effigy and toss it into the Tiber River to appease Tiberinus.

Tranquillitas is the goddess of peace, calmness, security, and tranquility. Her qualities are the embodiment of the Roman Way (Via Romana) and the justification for Rome to subdue, overcome and civilize the world around them.

Trivia is the goddess of magic, witchcraft, sorcery. She often frequented graveyards and haunted crossroads. Only barking dogs could see her as she wandered about at night.

The Creatures of Roman Mythology

The Romans did not contribute much in the way of mythological creatures. Their attempts at creating these creatures for their mythological world seem weak compared to the efforts of the Greeks.

Achlis is an elk-like creature with an upper lip so large the creature grazed backward to prevent the lip covering its mouth. In addition, Achlis' back legs have no joints, so it cannot sit down, and remains standing while sleeping. Frequently, it would be found leaning against a tree while resting. Hunters took advantage of this defect by cutting halfway through the tree against which the creature leaned. When the creature's weight forced the tree to topple, the creature could not get up fast enough to escape the hunters.

Cacus is a fire-breathing giant who terrorizes the people who live around the Aventine Hill before Rome is built. Cacus is a son of Vulcan who loved to eat human flesh. He was killed by Hercules (Greek Herakles).

Caladrius is a snow-white bird that lives in the house of the king. In Greek myth, this bird is called Dhalion. The bird benefited the king's household as it served as it could absorb the sickness of anyone who fell ill.

Faun is half-human and half-goat. The top half is human except for horns on their heads. Sometimes, they would help humans; at other times, they would hinder them. Fauns are sometimes confused with Greek satyrs.

Genius is similar to the Greek Daemon—a generalized divinity associated with every individual person. Sometimes, this creature is compared to the soul. Every place also had a spirit or soul—the genius loci, or spirit of a place.

Lemures are vengeful spirits who have not been properly buried. They manifested as a formless darkness and dread.

Strix are birds of ill omen who feed on flesh and blood of men. They have long beaks, are golden in color, with black talons, and round yellow eyes. They also suckled their young, which indicates they may have been bats and not birds.

Tarpeian Rock is an object in Roman legend that created a sufficient amount of horror in the minds of its citizens. All Roman traitors were thrown from this rock to their deaths.

The Romans were not imaginative when it came to mythological creatures. In the chapter on Greek gods, we will also look at some of the Greek mythological creatures adopted by the Romans.

Chapter 4 — Borrowings from Etruria

"Okay, you're so smart," said Kutu Lausa, "tell us why our capital was named for Menrva Velzna, but the Greeks got it all wrong, thinking her name was Pallas Athena." He lifted his cup to his mouth and took another swig of wine.

Tarquin Pulenas squinted, held his cup aloft for a thoughtful moment, then gulped his remaining wine. Ramtha, his wife, quickly refilled his cup.

Leaning forward, Tarquin looked at his guest and replied, "Yes, I am smart, but also quite aware of our shared histories. Menrva left the capital of Pos—the head city—taking with her hundreds of fellow refugees. She also took with her the knowledge of a mature society, the elements of weaving, furniture making, shipbuilding, fishing and other things basic to the art of civilization. She was fully equipped with the armaments to protect her fragile group, and they set up their outpost on Sherden Island across the Rasna Sea. We Rasenna are direct descendants of those who followed Menrva.

"When she built her capital, she used all her wisdom to reestablish the foundation of civilization.

Her beloved, who she thought had been killed, was actually alive and joined her in building their capital. The people were so overjoyed their savior could benefit from some happiness of her own, they requested the town be named in his honor.

"In the language of the day, towns were called 'pels.' And, because his name was Aten, the town was given the name, Pel es Atenai—Town of Aten."

"But wait," said Kutu, "that name sounds somewhat Egyptian."

"Very good, my friend," replied Tarquin. "It wasn't Egyptian, but because Menrva and Aten befriended the Egyptians against the Sett, Aten's name made its way into their legends.

"To continue, ages after Pel es Atenai had succumbed to the rising seas, the children of Menrva's refugees spread across the world, and some settled in what is today is the Greek homeland. Kekropna was a general of our people, and he led his men to sit on the Acropolis of Athens, long before it received that name. There, they debated what to name their new city. But look—the focus was on the name of a city—not a person."

Kutu nodded and bit his lower lip thoughtfully.

"Okay, now look at this fact: Pel es Atenai looks very much like the name these ignorant, modern-day Greeks attribute to their goddess—Pallas Athenai—borrowed from us, though they think they originated the legend. It came from us through General Kekropna. But again, they were naming not a person, but a city. So, they gave it a city's name—Pel es Atenai.

"They debated between Athenai and another great city named Pos. By that time, they had conflated two cities which had good relations, even unto the time of Menrva—Pos, and Onn—but the two cities were not even close to the same location. Later, because of the nature of Pos, they used its name for their god of the sea—Poseidon—Pos and Onn.

"So, finally: Our capital was named Velzna—Menrva's family name in the ancient homeland toward the setting sun. Our people had left this area in an earlier age, traveling to Anatolia. But after our capital there was destroyed by the Greeks, we returned to our ancient homeland to start again."

Kutu took another sip and shook his head. "That's all well and good, and I appreciate you filling in a lot of the missing pieces for me, but I've also heard that Menrva's lover was, in truth, named Apollo, instead of Aten."

Tarquin laughed so hard, the bench upon which he sat shook, rattling against the floor. After a moment, he regained his composure enough to speak again.

First, he held up his right hand to prevent any interruption and took another swig of wine from the cup in his left. Again, he chuckled softly and then spoke. "Yes, I've heard that, too. And it's true. Yet, Menrva was faithful to her Aten until the very end. Some of today's young people condemn this notion of her having a dalliance with this other fellow, Apollo—god of the sun. But it's quite simple.

"In Egypt, Aten was god of the sun. And in his own land, to distinguish Aten from the town after which he had been named, the citizens gave him a nickname—a name which meant quite literally 'not the pel.' Can you guess?"

Kutu shook his head slowly, uncertain how to respond. "Apollo?" he asked weakly.

Tarquin chuckled again. "Yes, my friend. A-pel-u—not the pel. He was also Apollo, god of the sun, poetry, prophecy, medicine, and agriculture."

Now, it was Kutu's turn to laugh. He did so, shaking his head. "Amazing how simple things are when you know the whole story behind all of the various details handed down as scraps in one Rasennan family or another. Very good. Very good, indeed."

From Rasenna

The Romans knew them as Etruscans and called their land Etruria. Today, it's called Tuscany. The Greeks called them Tyrrhenians—the name used for the sea west of Rome. To the people themselves, they were known as Rasenna or Rasna.

The following are some gods and goddesses who made their way from the Etruscan pantheon to that of the Romans.

Libitina is thought to be an Etruscan goddess of death, corpses, and funerals. Some scholars believe the name is taken from the Etruscan root, lupu-, which means "to die."

Minerva (Etruscan Menrva) is the goddess of wisdom who took on the traits and history of the Greek goddess Pallas Athena. As with Athena, Minerva was born from the head of Jupiter (Zeus) after the King of gods had swallowed her mother, Metis.

Orcus is the god of the underworld and punished those who did not live up to their oaths. Later, the Romans merged Orcus with Dis Pater, and then supplanted them with Pluto. Orcus provided the inspiration for J.R.R. Tolkien's orcs in his "Lord of the Rings" trilogy.

Volturnus is the god of water and the Tiber River. His festival is traditionally held on 27 August.

Chapter 5 — Influence of the Greek Pantheon

Flavius Secundus Iulius looked up at his father and frowned. After shaking his head for several seconds, he asked, "Why is it, father, that so many of our own gods sound like Greek gods? Not the names. No, that would be silly. But their descriptions—their attributes and accomplishments. Comparing Greek with Roman, they sound like the same gods, but with different names."

His father looked down at his son's large blue eyes and blond curls and smiled. He reached out and ruffled those curls, then winked.

Marcus Quintinus Iulius turned back to the plow shear he had been sharpening and continued to improve the blade with a sharpening stone.

"So?" said Flavius, as more of a demand than a question.

"Patience, my son," he replied, sliding the stone across the blade. "I'm thinking about the proper answer. You are wise to ask such a question, but not every answer will be so easily understood."

Flavius took a deep breath, let some of it out and said, "Yes, father."

The boy's slumped shoulders and down-turned mouth told his father the boy was not happy being patient. But even when the father had formulated an answer, he kept it to himself for several more, long seconds.

"Remember the hunt?" asked Marcus. "When you don't have patience…"

"…You can't catch game," Flavius repeated the well-worn lesson. He lifted his shoulders and let them down again, this time forcing them back. He sat more erect and compelled his lips to smile. "Yes, father."

Marcus laughed, a deep round noise that spoke of his pleasure with, and love of his son. "If you are in a crowd and someone your age calls out 'Iulius,' would you answer?"

"Possibly," he said, slowly, "if I were the only Iulius around."

"And," continued the father, "if someone else called out, 'Flavius,' would you answer them, as well?"

"In town, I suspect so," he replied, "since I'm the only Flavius that I know of."

"Fair enough." He gave his plow one more swipe with the sharpening stone, looked at the edge carefully and then set both the plow and the stone to one side. He turned to face his son squarely. "So, you would answer to two different names. And don't you have a nickname?"

"Father! Of course, I do. You've used it many times."

"Yes, I have. And it's a good one—Lex—meaning law or legal. So often you sound much like a legislator, with your logic. I'm proud of you, son."

Flavius nodded and looked away, suddenly distracted by his mother finishing the preparation for supper.

"So, Flavius Secundus Iulius Lex, you have a number of names that anyone could use to gain your attention."

"Yes, father. Even Secundus, on occasion."

"Very good. Now, the gods are very real. They have made their presence known to us, to the Greeks, to the Etruscans, and to many others, and they also have many names. To the Greeks, the founder of our family had the blood of Aphrodite flowing in his veins. To us, we call her 'Venus.' The goddess is the same. Different peoples merely have different names by which to call her."

Flavius nodded slowly, then hopped off his stool. Suddenly, he started pacing back and forth, hands tightly clasped behind his back. Then he stopped and stroked his chin, holding his elbow with his other hand, much as he had seen many a senator do in the capital. "So, Minerva is Athena; Jupiter is Zeus; Juno is Hera; Neptune is Poseidon, and Vulcan is Hephaestus."

His father nodded slowly and with a shallow, but certain movement. "We may not understand everything that the gods do, but if we uphold the nineteen virtues, that is the most the gods or any man can expect of us."

From the Greeks

Many of the gods we easily recognize as Roman may have been early Roman gods, but we have little documentation about them. Nearly everything we know about the following Roman gods has been intermingled with the stories and traits of their Greek counterparts.

Jupiter (Zeus) is king of the gods--God of sky, lightning, and thunder. He is the patron god of the Roman state. His nickname was Jove.

Juno (Hera) is the queen of the gods, wife, and sister to Jupiter, and sister to Neptune and Pluto, and protector of the Roman state. The month of June was named after her.

Minerva (Athena) is the goddess of wisdom. She was originally an Etruscan goddess but was given virtually all the attributes possessed by Athena—the ones that she did not already possess in Etruscan myth.

Neptune (Poseidon) is the god of the sea, horses, and earthquakes.

Pluto (Hades) is the god of the underworld and ruler of the dead.

Caelus (Uranus or Ouranos) is the god of the heavens.

Saturn (Cronus) is the god of time and harvests.

Vesta (Hestia) was the virgin goddess of home, hearth, and family.

Apollo (Apollo), son of Jupiter and Leto, twin brother of Diana, and god of music, archery, healing, light, truth, and prophecy. He was responsible for taking the sun across the sky.

Bacchus (Dionysus) is the god of grape harvesting, winemaking, wine, fertility, theater, religious ecstasy, and ritual madness. His followers were many, because of the emotional and drug-like hook of alcohol consumption and the enjoyable revelry of partying.

Ceres (Demeter) goddess of grain, agriculture, crops, initiation, civilization. She is the protector of motherhood, women, and marriage.

Cupid (Eros) is the god of desire, attraction, affection, and erotic love.

Diana (Artemis) is the goddess of fertility, the Moon, hunting, nature, childbirth, forests, animals, mountains, and women. She is a guardian of creatures.

Discordia (Eris) is the goddess of discord and strife. It was because of her the Trojan War happened, and Aeneas ended up in Italy.

Hercules (Herakles) is a demi-god or divine hero who had incredible strength and used his unique abilities on many incredible quests.

Latona (Leto) is a goddess, daughter of the Titans Coeus and Phoebe, consort of Zeus and mother of the twins, Apollo and Artemis. Because Juno (Hera) was extremely jealous of her husband's girlfriends and their children, the queen of the gods forbade any land from receiving Latona so she could give birth. Ultimately, she found an island which was not attached to the sea floor—technically not "land"—and thereupon gave birth to the divine twins.

Mars (Ares) was, early on, a god of agriculture, but then took on the responsibilities as the god of war. He is also the father of Romulus and Remus—founders of Rome.

Mercury (Hermes) is a god with many responsibilities, including, commerce, financial gain, messages, communication, eloquence in communication, poetry, divination, travelers, boundaries, thieves, trickery, and luck.

Proserpina (Persophone) is the goddess of grain and Queen of the dead. She is the daughter of Ceres. She was kidnapped by Pluto and forced into living in the underworld for a portion of the year. We have seasons because everything died when she was underground.

Venus (Aphrodite) is the goddess of mortal love. According to myth, she was born of sea foam created by the severed genitals of Uranus that his son Cronus threw into the sea.

Vulcan (Hephaestus) is the god of fire and metallurgy. He is frequently seen with his blacksmith's hammer. In fact, when Jupiter had a splitting headache, years after swallowing Metis whole, Vulcan used his hammer to whack Jupiter on the head, thus splitting the king's skull and allowing Minerva to step forth, full-grown (mature), and fully armored, holding weapons at the ready.

Lesser Gods and Goddesses

The following lesser-known gods and goddesses were the Roman version of the Greek deity.

Aesculapius (Asclepius) god of health and medicine.

Aurora (Eos) goddess of the dawn.

Concordia (Harmonia) goddess of agreement in marriage and society. She was frequently associated with Pax ("peace") and thus remained symbolic of a stable society.

Fama (Pheme) goddess of fame and rumor. If you were on her good side, you received renown and notability. If you ever made her angry, you were more likely to be plagued by scandalous rumor.

Faunus (Pan) horned god of animals, forest, plains, and fields. His wife was called Fauna, and she had similar attributes.

Flora (Chloris) a Sabine goddess of flowers and spring.

Formido (Deimos) god of dread or terror. See also Timorus. Both Formido and Timorus had their Greek versions used as the names of the planet Mars's two moons. After all, horror and dread are two common emotions felt during war, of which Mars was the god.

Fortuna (Tyche) goddess of fortune and luck. She is similar to Felicitas, but luck coming from Fortuna could sometimes be very negative.

Hespera (Hesperides) goddess of dusk. In Greek mythology, the name used refers to a group of evening nymphs and sunset's golden light.

Invidia (Nemesis, Rhamnusia or Adrasteia ["the inescapable"]) goddess of revenge, envy, jealousy, and retribution, especially against those who unwisely became arrogant—confident without humility—in the face of the gods.

Iris (Iris) goddess of the rainbow and a messenger of the gods.

Justitia (Themis or Dike) goddess of justice.

Luna (Selene) goddess of the Moon. In Roman mythology, both Juno and Diana were considered moon goddesses, and sometimes "Luna" was used not as a separate goddess, but as an epithet applied to the multi-talented Juno and Diana.

Maia (Maia) goddess of growth and the oldest of the seven sisters of the Pleiades.

Necessitas (Ananke) goddess of destiny, necessity, compulsion, and inevitability.

Opis (Rhea) goddess of fertility, named after the Sabine goddess, Ops. She was said to be the wife of Saturn and mother of the chief Roman gods—Jupiter, Neptune, Pluto, Juno, Ceres, and Vesta.

Pax (Eirene) goddess of peace.

Portunes (Palaemon) god of keys, doors, ports, and livestock. Some scholars believe he may also have been associated with warehouses where the Romans stored their grain. The connection to ports likely came from the similarity between the Latin words "portus" (harbor) and "porta" (door or gate). Harbors were, after all, gateways to the sea.

Sol (Helios) god of the sun. An early form of this god was called Sol Indiges. The later form, Sol Invictus ("unconquered sun"), seems to have come from Mithraic influences during the Roman Empire, especially after 274 AD.

Somnus (Hypnos) god of sleep.

Timorus (Phobos) god of fear or horror. See also Formido. Both Formido and Timorus had their Greek versions used as the names of the planet Mars's two moons. After all, horror and dread are two common emotions felt during war, of which Mars was the god.

Veritas (Aletheia) goddess of virtue and truth.

Victoria (Nike) goddess of victory.

Voluptas (Hedone) goddess of sensual pleasure and delight.

Greek Creatures Adopted by the Romans

The following is a list of many of the more widely known monsters and other creatures of Roman myth, focusing on those imported from the Greeks.

Caucasian Eagle is a large bird which was destined to eat the liver of Prometheus every day while he was chained to one of the Caucasus mountains.

Centaur is a half-horse and half-man. In effect, it had two torsos and six limbs. Most centaurs of ancient myth were wild and uneducated, but Chiron was a wise centaur who taught many of the legendary Greek heroes.

Cerberus is a three-headed dog which guarded the gates of Hades.

Charybdis is a massive whirlpool at a narrow strait between the island of Trinacria (Sicily) and the mainland peninsula (Italy). The narrow strait was dangerous for ships. If it is a ship got too close to one side, it might be swallowed by Charybdis. If it got too close to the other side, its crew might be snatched up by the Scylla.

Chimera is a complex, hybrid creature which combined the entire body of a lion with a neck and head of a goat coming out of the middle of its back, and a tail with a snake's head on its end.

Colchian Dragon is a fierce reptilian creature which had a serpent-like head and body, plus wings and feet. It stood in the gardens of Colchis guarding the Golden Fleece. It was finally vanquished by Jason and his Argonauts with the help of the Colchian princess, Medea.

Cyclopes are giant creatures of man-like form, but with only one eye in the center of each of their foreheads. There were two groups of these creatures. The relationship between these groups remains unknown. One set of three Cyclopes was born to Caelus (Uranus) and Terra (Gaia). They were imprisoned in the underworld but were rescued and freed by Jupiter. They were so grateful they fashioned three gifts, one each for Jupiter and his two brothers. For Jupiter, they created a lightning bolt. For Neptune, they fashioned a magical trident. And for Pluto, they hammered out a helmet that imparted invisibility to the wearer. The other Cyclopes were children of Neptune. The most famous Cyclops of this group was Polyphemus who ate some of Odysseus' men and was later blinded by Odysseus and his fellow survivors.

Echidna is a goddess who was half-woman and half-snake. She is the wife of Typhon and the mother of many monsters.

Gorgons are three monstrous sisters who are sometimes pictured with wings. Stheno and Euryale were immortal, but Medusa was not (see also, Medusa).

Graeae is a group of three witches who shared a single eye through which they possessed psychic and clairvoyant sight. The Greek demi-god Perseus consulted them when he was on his quest.

Hydra of Lerna (also called the Lernaean Hydra, or simply Hydra). This is a many-headed snake, child of Typhon and Echidna. Some versions of the myth include the creature's ability to regenerate two heads for every one cut off. Both its breath and blood were poisonous.

Medusa is one of the Gorgon monsters. Because Neptune had raped Medusa in the temple of Minerva, the goddess of wisdom condemned Medusa with a special curse which turned her hair into living, venomous snakes and her gaze into one which could turn men into stone.

Minotaur has the head of a bull and the body of a man. He lived in a labyrinth beneath the Minoan palace. He was slain by Theseus, the Athenian hero and illegitimate son of the king.

Nemean Lion could not be killed by mortal men or their weapons. Its golden fur was impervious to common blades. Its claws were strong and sharp enough to cut right through armor, making the creature a dangerous, formidable opponent. He is the offspring of Typhon and Echidna. Hercules found the Nemean Lion living in a cave with two entrances. He blocked one entrance and then went in the other to confront the monster. In the darkness, he grasped the creature, and with his great strength, crushed the lion's neck, strangling it. To get proof of his conquest, Hercules attempted to skin the lion with his knife and then with a sharp rock, but neither one worked. Minerva saw his struggling and told him to use one of the lion's own claws to skin the beast which worked.

Scylla is a monster with six long necks, each equipped with a gruesome head with lots of sharp teeth. Her parents were Typhon and Echidna. She stood on one shore of the narrow strait between the island of Trinacria (Sicily) and the mainland peninsula (Italy), posing a danger to sailors. The narrow strait was dangerous for ships because if a ship got too close to one side, its crew might be snatched up by the Scylla. If it got too close to the other side, it might be swallowed by Charybdis (see Charybdis, also).

Sphinx is a creature with the head of a woman, the body of a lion, and the wings of an eagle. She blocked the road to travelers insisting they answer her riddle. If they answered incorrectly, she would devour them. When Greek tragic hero, Oedipus encountered the Sphinx, the riddle most often quoted went like this: "What is that which in the morning goeth upon four feet; upon two feet in the afternoon; and in the evening upon three?" Oedipus realized only a man does these things—first crawling on all fours as an infant, then walking on two legs as an adult, and finally using a cane as an old man. The Sphinx was so shocked someone had answered the riddle correctly; she devoured herself in her anguish.

Typhon is the son of Terra (Gaia) and Tartarus (Tartarus). He is the father, with Echidna, of many monsters. He challenged Jupiter for rule over the universe, after Jupiter, and his fellow gods had defeated the Titans.

Chapter 6 — Celtic Potpourri

Boudicca (30-61 AD) is a middle-aged woman of noble birth wronged by the Roman Empire.

Her late husband was King of the Iceni in Britannia. When he died, he left his kingdom to three parties—his two daughters and the Roman Emperor. But the Romans ignored the will because they believed women were not allowed to possess property.

Gaius Suetonius Paulinus, the Roman governor of the Empire's British holdings, simply annexed the Iceni territory. When Boudicca protested, she was flogged, and her daughters were raped.

But now, Governor Paulinus was away, claiming new territory for the Empire off the coast of Wales.

Behind Boudicca was a force of over 100,000 men and women, from her own tribe, from the Trinovantes, and from many others.

She wiped her upper lip, carefully with the back of her hand. Exertion and this sweltering, summer had her sweating profusely. Britannia during the Roman Warm Period was measurably warmer than in modern times. She lightly touched the gold torc wrapped around her neck—a symbol of royal authority amongst her people. The rigid neck ring was intricately decorated with symbols representing the spirits. On the front of her torc, where the two ends met, one end was embossed with the tiny image of three women—the máthair or matronae. The other end had embossed a tiny image of Epona—the horse goddess, and goddess of fertility.

She should not have to fight to restore the birthright of her two daughters, but they had been cheated by the patriarchal Romans. But here she was, leading a massive army toward Londinum—a settlement only 20 years old. Her forces destroyed Camulodunum, a Roman settlement that was rebuilt and called Colchester.

She looked back as she heard the others approach. The old man was Haerviu—too long in years to live up to his name "battle worthy." He was an adviser of hers and surprisingly had survived the war so far.

Lugubelenus was a brash young man who had already made several advances against one of her daughters and fancied himself as a leader. What he lacked in wisdom he made up for with fierce skills as a warrior and a deep humility to the gods.

Teutorigos was the last to arrive. His name meant "ruler of the people," and he had great potential but little interest in such power. His brand of humility was not the righteous kind, but more of a weak lack of ambition. A worthy Celt needed to maintain strong confidence, but with a deep humility to the gods and their laws.

"By Epona," she whispered loudly. "What have you found out?"

"Londinum is empty," replied Teutorigos quietly. "They've abandoned it."

"Apparently, they did not think their auxiliary forces could hold the settlement," said Haerviu. "I sincerely doubt the liars merely had a change of heart and decided to honor the will of their supposed friend, the late king."

"We should burn the settlement, nonetheless." Lugubelenus glanced at Boudicca and lifted his chin a bit.

"For once, I agree with Lugubelenus," replied Boudicca. "Punish these thieves in every way we can, but more importantly, force them to spend time rebuilding, if they desire to keep this Londinum. If the gods smile on us, perhaps the Romans will get the idea that holding this island is too much trouble."

"May Cernunnos guide us," said Haerviu. "We don't do these things for our own selfish needs, but for the greater good of the natural world, of which we are a part."

"Well said, as always, Haerviu," replied Boudicca. "May the three mothers protect us in what we are about to do. Teutorigos, send our scouts to the West. Make certain the governor isn't going to surprise us. Lugubelenus, take ten thousand men into Londinum and set it ablaze."

"Yes, my queen," said Lugubelenus.

Despite their successes, so far, Boudicca secretly feared Roman power. With such a vast, organized empire, her people could easily be overwhelmed by their millions. She prayed to the gods her people would prevail. But sometimes prayer was not enough.

Roman Conquests of the Celts

The Romans kept running into Celtic peoples—from Gallia and Britannia to Illyrium and Galatia. Roman expansion meant they encountered the Celts on almost every front, for over three centuries.

The **Matres and Matronae** were, across most of the Celtic world, worshipped throughout the period of the Roman Empire. Almost always, they were depicted on altars and votive offerings as a group of three goddesses—the "mother" goddesses. These divine beings were similar in some respects to the dísir and the valkyries of Norse mythology, as well as the Fates of Greek mythology. Dea Matrona means "divine mother goddess" and this name was sometimes used in place of Matres and Matronae. Dea Matrona was also the source name for the river Marne in Gaul.

Toutatis is considered a tribal protector for the Celts of Gaul and Britain. In Roman Britain, finger rings with the initials "TOT" were common and were thought to refer to the god Toutatis. Some scholars believe the Romans associated Toutatis with their own Mercury. In fact, Julius Caesar said that "Mercury" was their most esteemed god and that images of him were to be found throughout the Celtic territory. To the Celtic "Mercury" were attributed the functions of "inventor of all the arts," protector of merchants and travelers, and the preeminent god for everything concerning commercial gain. Toutatis could have been one member of a triune god named Lugus.

Caesar studied the Celts intensely because he wanted to conquer them. He also mentioned that the Celts of Gaul paid homage to Apollo because he rid them of diseases. They honored Mars, who ruled over all the things of war. They revered Jupiter, who oversaw the heavens. And they honored Minerva, who remained patroness of handicrafts. Julius Caesar also mentioned the Celtic Gauls all claimed to be descended from Dīs Pater, which was a Roman god of the underworld. Likely what he meant was that the Gauls claimed to be from a god who resembled Dīs Pater in some way—perhaps a subterranean god associated with prosperity and fertility.

Aerecura (see Erecura).

Aisus (see Esus).

Alaunus is a god of healing and prophecy which are two of the traits held by Apollo, both in the Greek and Roman pantheons.

Alisanos may have been a mountain god or may have been related to the alder tree.

Andarta is a warrior goddess with evidence of her worship in Bern, Switzerland and in southern France.

Anextiomarus (female form, Anextiomara) has been associated with the Roman god Apollo, with dedications found throughout France and Switzerland.

Artio is a bear goddess. Her worship was centered on Bern, Switzerland.

Aveta is a mother goddess worshipped across a region which includes parts of France, Germany, and Switzerland.

Belenus is a sun god, associated with horses, and thought to ride across the sky in a horse-drawn chariot, pulling the sun along with it. His consort is Celtic goddess Belisama, who is frequently associated with Minerva.

Borvo is a god involved in healing, minerals, and bubbling spring water. Whenever associated with a Roman god, Borvo was always paired with Apollo.

Brigantia is associated with Roman Victoria and remains a cognate with Irish Brigit.

Camulus is another Celtic god associated with Mars. In one stone carving, he is portrayed with a wreath of oak. In another location, he is shown with a ram head wearing horns. His name may have been the basis of Camelot—the legendary city of King Arthur fame. Many theories have been offered about the possible reality of King Arthur, but there is no way to verify them with the current evidence.

Cathubodua is a Celtic goddess and possible cognate of Irish Babd Catha. Her name meant "battle crow." Several goddesses share the same root which means either "victory" or "fighting." Because of this, she would be comparable to goddesses in other cultures—Victoria (Roman), Nike (Greek) and Sigyn (Norse).

Cernunnos is a horned god of life, fertility, wealth, animals and the realm of the underworld. He is shown with stag antlers, sometimes carrying a coin purse. Most of the time he is seen seated cross-legged. He is also shown wearing torcs or holding them in his hands.

Cicolluis is the "Great-Breasted" god of strength, associated with Mars. This god has sometimes been associated with Cichol Gricenchos of Irish Celtic myth.

Cissonius is yet another Celtic god associated with Mercury. In attempting to understand his name, linguists have interpreted it as meaning "carriage-driver" or "courageous." From this, they suspect he is a god of trade and patron protector of those who traveled. Thus, the association with Mercury seems to be a good fit. There is also a minor note of a goddess named Cissonia, but the relationship to this god is unknown.

Condatis—a name which means "waters meet"—is a Celtic god related to rivers, especially where they come together. He is associated with the Roman god Mars, likely through his divine healing powers.

Damona is a Celtic goddess. According to one scholar, her name means "divine cow"—from Celtic "damos" which means "cow." In two different regions, she was seen with a divine consort—Apollo Borvo in one, and Apollo Moritasgus in another.

Epona is a goddess of fertility, plus a protector of horses, ponies, donkeys, and mules. The Roman spelling was sometimes Hippona. She was one of the most broadly worshipped of any Celtic god. Some scholars feel she may have been associated with the dead, leading them to the "otherworld" on a pony. Evidence of her worship has been found in Britain, throughout Gaul, modern Germany and the Roman provinces of the River Danube. One inscription in Germany was made by someone from the region of ancient Syria.

Erecura (also spelled Aerecura) a Celtic goddess associated with the Roman goddess of the underworld, Proserpina (Greek Persophone). Evidence of her worship has been found in modern Belgium, southeastern France, southwestern Germany, eastern Austria, northeastern Italy and central Romania. Along with her symbols of the underworld, she is frequently seen with a cornucopia or an apple basket—symbols of fertility. Though the Celts revered this goddess across a broad territory, scholars doubt the name was, in fact, Celtic. One researcher suggested the name was originally Illyrian.

Esus (also spelled Hesus and Aisus) is a Celtic god. He was depicted cutting branches from a willow tree with his blade. One intellectual suggests that his name derives from the Indo-European root for "well-being, passion, and energy." The willow tree may represent the "Tree of Life." He could have been one part of a triune God, Lugus.

Grannus is a Celtic god of spas—healing mineral and thermal springs. He was also associated with the sun, and thus frequently associated with Apollo as Apollo Grannus. His worship was also frequently associated with Celtic Sirona and sometimes Roman Mars. Perhaps the most famous center for worshipping Grannus can be found near the modern city of Aachen, Germany, that country's westernmost municipality. In ancient times, the hot springs there was called Aquae Granni. Roman Emperor Caracalla (AD 188–217) was said to have visited there with votive offerings and prayers to be healed.

Hesus (see Esus).

Ialonus Contrebis (or Ialonus and Gontrebis) was either a Celtic god or two gods. The first part—Ialonus—seems to come from a root meaning "clearing."

Lenus is the Celtic god of healing, frequently associated with Roman god Mars. He was particularly important to the Treveri tribe in what is now western Germany. Unlike most syncretized names combining Celtic with Roman divinity, most inscriptions show "Lenus Mars," rather than "Mars Lenus." Quite often, he is pictured wearing a Greek Corinthian helmet.

Litavis (also Litauis) is a Celtic goddess sometimes associated with the Gallo-Roman syncretized god, Mars Cicolluis, suggesting she may have been his consort. Some scholars consider her to be an earth goddess with a name derived from language roots meaning "to spread out flat."

Loucetios is a Celtic god whose name means "lightning." He was invariably associated with Mars as Mars Loucetios and frequently associated with the goddess Gallic Nemetona or Roman Victoria. He was known throughout the Rhine River Valley region, from Austria and Switzerland, through Germany, France, Liechtenstein and the Netherlands. Inscriptions to this god have also been found in Angers, western France and in Bath, England.

Lugus is a Celtic god whose name remains a cognate with the Irish god Lugh. Though his name is rarely mentioned directly, his importance is implied by the proliferation of place names which seem to pay homage to him. His name seems to come from the Proto-Indo-European roots "to break" and "to swear an oath." A three-headed image found in Paris and Reims was thought to represent Lugus and is associated with the Roman god Mercury. Linguists suggest his name was the basis for the following location names:

- Dinlleu, Wales
- Legnica, Silesia
- Leiden, Netherlands
- Lothian, Scotland
- Loudoun, Scotland
- Loudun and Montluçon in France
- Lugdunum (modern Lyon, France)
- Lugones, Asturias, Spain
- Luton, England

One scholar suggests Lugus was a triune God, as represented by the three-headed image, representing Esus, Toutatis, and Taranis.

Maponos is a Celtic god with a name that meant "great son." He was equated with Roman Apollo.

Mogons is a Celtic god frequently adopted by common Roman soldiers in Roman Britain and Gaul. Linguists suggest its meaning derives from roots for "effective" or "powerful."

Nantosuelta is a Celtic nature goddess of fire, earth, and fertility. She is thought to have been part of the Irish Tuatha Dé Danann, combined with Sucellus and subsequently with Dagda. Some evidence suggests hers was the name assumed by The Morrígan after a joining of new alliances or a transformation. Her name literally means, "sun-drenched valley" or "of winding stream."

Ogmios is a Celtic god of persuasiveness. His name remains a cognate with the Irish god Ogma. He is described as an older version of Herakles, the Greek demigod of great strength. Like Herakles, Ogmios wore a lion skin and carried a club and bow. In his Celtic version, however, he is seen with chains piercing his tongue, flowing from his mouth and out to the ears of his happy followers.

Ritona (also Pritona) was a Celtic goddess of "water crossings" or "fords." Her temples seemed to have more extras than do many of the other gods—like courtyards which could easily have been used for the placement of ritual offerings or the preparation of religious banquets. Another such temple even had a theater, supposedly for religious performances.

Rosmerta is a Celtic goddess of abundance and fertility. Her image is often found alongside the Roman god Mercury as if she were his consort. She was worshipped from central France to western Germany.

Segomo is a Celtic war god whose name meant "mighty one" or "victor." Naturally, he is associated with the Roman god, Mars, but also with Hercules.

Sirona is a Celtic goddess throughout Gaul but also worshipped as far east as the Danube River. She has been associated with the Roman goddess, Diana.

Sucellus is a Celtic god frequently depicted with Nantosuelta. He is usually seen carrying a large hammer or mallet, which could easily have been a beer barrel on a long pole.

Suleviae was a group of Celtic goddesses whose name meant "those who govern well." This group was sometimes associated with the Matres. In fact, one inscription starts out, "To the Sulevi mothers…"

Taranis is a Celtic god of thunder. One curious coincidence ties Taranis with the Greek cyclops Brontes (whose name meant "thunder") because both were associated with a wheel. Some scholars suggest that Taranis was not so much a god of thunder as he was actually the thunder itself. His worship spanned a broad territory including Gaul, Britain, parts of former Yugoslavia and modern Germany. Lucan, the Roman poet, called Taranis a "savage god" who required human sacrifice. Taranis also remains a cognate with the Irish god Tuirenn. Taranis could also have been part of a triune God, Lugus. Because of his association with thunder or identity as thunder, he is also associated with the Roman god Jupiter, the Greek god Zeus, and the Norse god Thor.

Virotutis is a Celtic byname given the Roman god, Apollo. It meant, "benefactor of humanity." Apollo Virotutis was worshipped just south of Switzerland and in western France.

Visucius is a Celtic god whose name meant "knowledgeable" or "of the ravens." He was usually associated with the Roman god, Mercury, and was worshipped from western Germany to northern Spain.

Other Borrowed Gods

One goddess which was actively sought out by the Romans was the Phrygian Great Mother, Cybele. The assimilation of this goddess had nothing to do with conquest. During the Second Punic War (218–201 BC), the Romans suffered one setback after another. Several natural events were taken as signs of imminent failure in their war against the Carthaginians. One of those signs was a meteor shower, which the ancients always took as a bad omen, even though their enemies were very likely to have seen the same sign. Another involved a failed harvest and resulting famine. But that was merely a natural occurrence of climate change, cooling the planet between warm periods. There was a particularly sharp drop in temperature, measured in the Greenland ice cores indicative of a northern hemisphere cooling period that lasted several years during the time of the Second Punic War. But despite these things, the Romans were persistent and insistent.

After consulting the Sibylline oracle, Rome's religious advisers came up with a unique answer to their problem. If they could legally import the Magna Mater (Cybele) of Pessinos, Phrygia (west-central Anatolia, or modern-day Turkey), they would be able to regain the favor of the gods.

In Rome's favor, the home of worship of this "Great Mother," was at the center of one of their allies—the Kingdom of Pergamum.

Immediately, the Roman Senate sent emissaries to gain the king's approval for Rome to import the goddess. These emissaries stopped by the Oracle at Delphi to confirm they were doing the right thing and received the confirmation they sought—that the goddess should be taken back to Rome.

To make the transference official, the King of Pergamum gave his Roman friends a black meteoric stone which was symbolic of the goddess. In a great ceremony full of pomp, the stone was met at Rome's seaport at Ostia and escorted by Rome's "best man," Publius Cornelius Scipio Nasica, along with an entourage of virtuous matrons to take the stone back to the temple of Victoria to be stored, while a more rightful temple of the Great Mother was being built on the Palatine Hill.

Not long afterward, the famine ended, and the Romans were victorious against Hannibal and the Carthaginians.

One of the most important gods which the Romans borrowed from cultures other than the Etruscans, Greeks or Celts, was the Persian god, **Mithra**—renamed Mithras by the Greeks, and worshipped by Imperial soldiers. The citizens-at-large knew about the worship, but the adherents kept their rituals and prayers a secret. Roman Mithraism was a "mystery religion," full of symbolism and secrecy. They did not need or want new members. They had a special handshake, plus an intricate system of seven levels for the various stages of initiation. Some rituals involved the killing of a bull. To its adherents, each ritual symbolized the struggle between good and evil, and of the sacrifice that is sometimes required. Roman Mithraism presented strong competition for early Christianity.

In 312 AD, at the Battle of Milvian Bridge, Constantine the Great (c.272–337 AD) had a decisive win, the success of which he later attributed to the **Christian God.** After that battle, he converted to Christianity and placed the Christian God ahead of all others.

After nearly two centuries of brutal persecution, the Christian religion had become the dominant religion in the Roman Empire. Because of Constantine's conversion, Europe became predominantly Christian.

Chapter 7 — Truth Behind the Roman Gods

While we may never know the actual truth behind each Roman god and goddess, we should acknowledge there is some unknown truth that may well remain unrecorded by any history, as with any myth. What do we mean by this? At the very least, the gods may have been created to explain physical or social phenomena. This is one possibility.

Another possible truth is that a god or goddess may have been an ancient king, queen, hero or heroine.

Still another possibility holds that some of the gods and goddesses of myth were groups, instead of individuals. At least one other researcher has put forth this idea, and we should remain open to this possibility.

To primitive hunter-gatherers, the name of an empire might have been a mystery because they didn't have any concept of "empire." It's easy to see how such a name might have become transformed into a god or goddess. It's also easy to see how the many traits of a god may merely have been the talents collectively held by a group, especially if the hunter-gatherers suffered from the power of the empire.

For example, we trust those in authority. But for over a thousand years in Europe, those in authority did not consider challenging their ideas about the universe. Even today, non-traditional ideas are discounted, ignored, or even ridiculed simply because they don't fit some current consensus. Simply because an idea is popular doesn't make it right. For example, scientists of the 19th century felt Homer's *Iliad* was purely myth with little basis in fact.

Scientists felt that Troy was pure myth simply because they had known of no evidence to the contrary. While this conclusion from a lack of evidence is value, it should not present pursuing further exploration. The pursuit of evidence of Troy did, in fact, lead to the discovery of Troy.

It is possible that pursuit of the truth underlying myths could lead to challenges to the prevailing religious understanding.

As we saw earlier, the Etruscans have a genetic relationship to the people who currently live in what is modern Turkey (ancient Anatolia or Asia Minor). The Etruscans may have been descendants of

Aeneas and the Trojans, or at least the people who lived in and around Troy, They may, therefore, have been distant relatives of Romulus and Remus. Was Etruscan the language of the Trojans, or a derivative of their language? As far as we know, the Trojans did not employ writing, so we cannot prove such an idea. But an inability to prove an idea doesn't make it false. It simply remains an unknown.

One researcher—Rod Martin, Jr.—discovered a linguistic link between Etruscan (Rasennan) and Basque (Eskual), albeit a weak one. The nature of the link suggests both cultures may have been matriarchal at one time. The most sentimentally favorite words in any language may arguably be "mother" and "father." Basque for father is "aita," while mother is "ama." Etruscan for father was "apa," while mother was "ati." This, by itself, seems very weak, indeed, and the terms seem to be gender opposites. But as we saw earlier, the Etruscan goddess of beginnings was "Ana," while the god of endings was "Aita." These match the Basque terms almost perfectly by gender.

Martin suggests both cultures may have been matriarchal in prehistory. As more patriarchal societies entered Europe, peer pressure may have affected a desire to switch.

"What? You let your women rule? You must be weak!" would be the attitude of a patriarchal society. If a patriarchal tribe judged a matriarchal society as weak, they might continue to attack that society. Weary of being attacked, a matriarchal society might switch to change the perception of their enemies.

Both Greek and Roman cultures viewed the Etruscans with disdain, even though the Etruscans were patriarchal because they gave their women so much power and allowed them to own property. But what if, instead, it was the women who gave their men the power?

In analyzing the two languages, Martin realized both were agglutinative. That by itself proves little. But he suggests the Basques switched to patriarchy and kept the terms for mother and father with the same gender always attached to those terms. However, the Etruscans kept the terms with the societal roles. Their rulers had been mothers and men became the new mothers—"apa," or two letter "a's" separated by a labial sound ("p"), just as Basque for mother—"ama"—is also two letter "a's" separated by the labial "m." The names of their god and goddess of endings and beginnings may hold the clue to the gender switch, because Basque for father, "aita," is exactly the same as the Etruscan male god for endings, "Aita." And Basque for mother, "ama," is almost the same as the Etruscan female goddess for beginnings, "Ana."

How valid is this analysis? Even Martin acknowledges this is a hypothesis which needs additional support. But one other culture may validate this notion of a matriarchal society switching to patriarchy and keeping the terms with the role rather than the gender. Another agglutinative language—Georgian (Kartuli ena)—may have experienced a similar phenomenon. Today, Georgian for mother is "deda," and father is "mama."

Georgia, at the eastern end of the Black Sea, was at one time called Colchis—the kingdom which held the Golden Fleece and a golden dragon to protect it. Were the Georgians related in some way to the Trojans, Etruscans, and therefore the Basques? Linguists of the 19th century felt the similarities between Basque and Georgia were strong enough to consider the possibility they were descended from the same tongue. Both regions have also been called "Iberia," even though they are separated by thousands of kilometers. As tantalizing as the possibilities are, we need to use restraint and remind ourselves we simply do not know. Today, linguists tell us the evidence linking the two languages is too tenuous to prove a link. But again, a lack of evidence is never proof against a thesis. It only means we need more evidence.

In the final analysis, we may never have conclusive answers to our questions of divine beginnings. The Roman family of gods was perhaps one of the largest of all ancient pantheons simply because they absorbed the gods and goddesses of the peoples they conquered.

But what about the creatures of myth. Was there some basis in reality for them, as well, or were they all based purely on imagination? Consider, for instance, what a primitive man might think of someone wearing a flight suit or astronaut's spacesuit. Would the faceplate of their helmet be thought of as "one eye," making them a Cyclops?

Some researchers believe centaurs were merely the result of primitive shock and awe at seeing a normal man riding horseback. In their imagination, they saw only the human torso and head, and horse body. Having never seen the combination of horse and rider, the primitive mind attempted to process the image in the only way it could—imagining they had witnessed a new kind of creature.

Could the faun merely have been a soldier with furry leggings and leather boots, wearing a helmet with horns? These are possibilities, but with no way to know for certain.

And such is the nature of any myth. Its beginnings remain shrouded in the mists of prehistory.

Conclusion - What We've Learned

I hope this book has helped you to gain a fresh perspective of the Romans and an overview of their gods, goddesses, and mythological creatures.

In the introduction, we learned that the Romans were a serious lot. Though they were not very creative, they did have many virtues, including the fact that they were hard working and were clever at using well the resources available to them. We learned that they were originally farmers and that their gods had a lot to do with rain and crops.

Chapter 1, "The Trojan Connection," gave us a look at Aeneas and how one goddess, in particular, hated the Trojan and the survivors of the Trojan War. We also gained historical context of the Roman myth of Aeneas.

In chapter 2, "Founding of Rome," we got an intimate look at the founding of that great city by Romulus and Remus. We also learned how tiny Rome was surrounded by dozens of other tribes, each vying for supremacy or merely trying to survive.

Chapter 3, "Purely Roman Gods," showed us the early Roman kingdom and the celebration of the river god, Tiberinus. We also saw a list of Roman gods, many of which were likely unfamiliar to the casual student of history. And we saw a few of the awkwardly unimaginative creatures from Roman myth.

In "Borrowings from Etruria" (chapter 4), we looked at the gods and goddesses contributed by Rome's vastly larger neighbor to the North—Rasenna, or as the Romans knew them—Etruria. Our narrative took a fanciful look at one possible interpretation for how the various pantheons may have fit together. We also saw how the Etruscans might have been more closely related to the Romans than we've been led to believe, with their ancestors possibly having come from Troy along with Aeneas. And we learned of a few gods and goddesses which contributed to the Roman pantheon.

Perhaps the greatest foreign contribution to Roman mythology came from the Greeks. In chapter 5, "Influence of the Greeks," we saw how nearly all of the most well-known Roman gods and goddess were largely Greek gods which were restyled as Roman. And we saw how the richest list of Roman mythical creatures was populated with names borrowed from the Greeks. This should not surprise us, for to the Romans, Greek myth had merely become part of their own history.

In chapter 6, we learned how the Celts contribute a great deal of their own mythology to the Romans. With the Celtic pantheon, Roman gods and goddesses now took on composite names which combined Roman and Celtic elements.

Finally, in chapter 7, we explored some of the possible origins of the gods and goddesses.

Preview of Norse Mythology

A Captivating Guide to Norse Folklore Including Fairy Tales, Legends, Sagas and Myths of the Norse Gods and Heroes

Introduction

Before Christianity reached what we now call Europe, the Germanic people of that region—people whom we now call Vikings-- had their own sacred stories and practices. Scholars say they didn't share one carefully threshed-out canon of agreed sacred texts; rather, the stories passed from teller to teller, and were different in different regions and different times. The gods celebrated in those stories were also many, varied, and often at variance. Sometimes their deeds and words were high and solemn, full of noble self-sacrifice; sometimes they were mischievous or short-sighted. In this, perhaps, they were like the people who listened to the stories, who laughed and wept and remembered.

The stories linger in our culture today. Four days of our week are named after members of the Norse pantheon (Tyr, Woden (Odin), Thor and Frigg). Wagner's Ring Cycle has kept one version of one of the great Norse stories alive in the minds of music lovers. Readers of modern fantasy will find many echoes of the Norse tales as well. Neil Gaiman, Douglas Adams and others have explicitly taken some of the Norse gods and put them into a modern setting with strange, sad and humorous results. Echoes of Norse tales and creatures abound in the speculative fiction of Ursula Le Guin, J.R.R. Tolkien, C.S. Lewis, Tad Williams and others. Something in these old and puzzling stories still has the power to move and unsettle us, and to inspire new acts of creation.

This book will give you a brief introduction to some of the best-known myths found in the primary sources. Suggestions for further reading are offered in the conclusion. There's a glossary of names in the back in case you need help keeping track of a rather large cast of characters. Enjoy your explorations!

Chapter 1 – The Creation of the Worlds

The world began, as it would end, in fire. From the primordial chaos which held neither day nor night, sea nor land, life nor death, a spark arose. The flame, feeding on its own hunger, raged and spread and became the bright hot world of Muspelheim, a living furnace which poured rivers of fire and blasts of hot air into the surrounding void.

Once heat and light existed, their opposites also came into being. Across the universe from Muspelheim another world took shape: Niflheim, icebound, dark and deadly cold. From Niflheim a venomous chilling wind poured into the void, and a slow river of grinding ice.

Ice and fire met in the emptiness. There were terrible explosions, and the void was filled with flying sparks and shards of shattered ice, with fountains of water and jets of steam. That collision birthed the frost-giant Ymir. He was strong and cold and deadly as the breath of Niflheim, but he had the fire-spark of life in him. Ymir sweated as the sparks flew around him, and from the sweat-drops new giants came to life.

Ymir and his brood were not the only ones born of the ice-melt. The cow Audhumbla also took shape between fire and ice, and Ymir and his children drank her milk. She also was thirsty, and she quenched her thirst by licking the ice. Something new began to emerge under the strokes of her tongue: first what looked like a man's hair emerged, and then a head, and then the whole figure stepped free of the ice and looked about him. His name was Buri, and he was the first of the gods. Buri was as beautiful as he was strong, and he wanted others of his own kind. He made his own son, Borr. Borr loved the giantess Bestla, and she bore sons, of whom the greatest was Odin.

Odin and his brothers fought Ymir. The war was remembered long after the reasons were forgotten. Maybe the giant didn't approve of his offspring marrying gods instead of one another. Maybe both Odin and Ymir wanted to claim the whole world for their own people. Be that as it may, they fought, and Odin and his brothers won. Ymir fell dead in the void between the world of fire and the world of ice, and Ymir's blood rose in a great flood and drowned the other frost-giants—all but the giant Bergelmir and his wife. While the others fought, Bergelmir had built a great ship, and as the flood rose he and his wife went into their ship and rode the blood-tide to a safe place beyond the reach of the young gods.

Odin and his brothers turned from fighting to building. They took Ymir's body and reshaped it into a world, a flat ring set midway between the worlds of ice and fire, in a place of flowing water and mild air. Ymir's icy blood became the world's lakes and seas, his flesh and bones the land and the mountains. His skull was set up above the world, becoming the arch of the sky. The gods took fire from the sparks of Muspelheim and threw them into the air beneath that arch to give light to the world. On the outer margins of that world, beside the endless sea that marked its boundary, was a wasteland inhabited by Bergelmir's children and their children, the giants who remembered Ymir's death and waited for their chance to avenge it. But in the middle of the world the gods raised a defensive wall, built from Ymir's eyebrows, to keep the giants at bay. This defended land was called Midgard, the world of men.

Here, after chaos and war, there was rest and order and the beginning of another kind of life. The sun warmed the earth. Green plants sprang up and grew. Odin and his brothers took two trees, shaped them in the image of the gods, breathed life into their flesh and inspiration into their souls. Ask was the first man, and Embla the first woman, and from those two came all the people of the world.

The gods also took the maggots that gnawed Ymir's flesh, gave them a humanlike form and breathed wisdom into them. These became the race of dwarves, who shared the world with humans, not always happily... As we shall see in other tales.

Notes to the Creation Story:

Like most of the Norse myths, the creation story exists in several forms. It's told in fragments scattered through several of the ancient texts called the Poetic Eddas (most notably in "Voluspa" and "Hovamol,") and in one coherent chunk by twelfth-century statesman and writer Snorri Sturluson in *Gylfaginning*, the first half of the Prose Edda. Snorri drew on the Poetic Eddas, and on some other sources that are lost to us now. He also made some puzzling attempts to harmonize the Norse myths with Christianity, and with Greek mythology; I've left some of those features out. If you're interested in reading the originals, English translations of all the Eddas are available free online.

But the details may vary, the Norse myths agree that the world was born in chaos, and was from its beginning made up of warring opposites: heat and cold, ice and fire, giants and gods. The world was made by the gods from the body of their enemy. Odin himself, the leader of the gods against the giants, was the son of a giantess. There was glory and courage and beauty in the world of the Norse myths, but there was not very much peace.

Chapter 2 – The Building of Asgard

After shaping Midgard for mortals, the gods made a splendid city for themselves and named it Asgard. It was bound to the earth by the fiery bridge called Bifrost, the rainbow; the gods hoped that the giants would be unable to cross this bridge and attack them. Living humans could not pass that way either. But warriors who died bravely in battle were taken up by the Valkyries, the fierce and beautiful daughters of Odin, to Asgard. Half of them went to Odin's castle called Valhalla, where they spent their days in fighting each other (not in hostility, but for practice and for the joy of battle; every evening the injured were restored to perfect health) and their nights in feasting. The other half went to Folkvangr, the great hall of Odin's wife Frigg. Frigg was the wisest of the goddesses. She watched over, and had the power to alter the magical weaving which determined the fates of mortals. Sometimes, unlike her husband, she took brave women as well as brave men into her hall.

All the buildings of Asgard were made of gold. Splendor was everywhere. So were endless life and unwithering strength, thanks to the goddess Iduna's apple tree whose fruit made the eater immortal. And in one place there was something rarer than splendor or immortality—peace. That was in Breiddablik, the Peace Stead, the palace of Balder. Balder was so beautiful that he shed light where he walked, and his judgments were so wise and just that his quarrelsome fellow gods did not find fault with them.

In the midst of all this beauty Odin was uneasy. He remembered the anger of the giants, and he feared that they would destroy everything he and his brothers and sisters had created. The warriors in Valhalla fought each other daily so that they would be a formidable force whenever the day of reckoning came, but he didn't trust that army to save him from the forces the giants could raise. He often went to his other castle Valaskjalf, whose topmost tower was so high that he could see any place in the Worlds from it; he sat alone there, looking, pondering, worrying.

But the first threat to Asgard came, not from the giants, but from another race of gods, the Vanir. Nobody remembers now where the Vanir came from; perhaps they were descended from Buri or Borr's other children. Be that as it may, the Aesir (Asgard's inhabitants) and the Vanir saw each other's power from afar off, felt threatened, and attacked each other. The fighting was long and equally matched; the Vanir threw down the walls of Asgard, but they could not drive the Aesir out. Finally, weary of war and each impressed by the courage and strength of the others, they decided to make a treaty of peace. The Vanir withdrew to their own lands. Two of the Aesir went with them as hostages or ambassadors, and they soon passed out of the stories of the North. Three of the Vanir remained as hostages in Asgard: Njord, god of the sea and sailors, his son Frey, and his daughter Freya. Now Freya was a wise-woman, skilled in seeing the future, and she had a set of falcon feathers which allowed the wearer to take bird-shape and fly. She was also devastatingly beautiful and free with her favors to any god who struck her fancy.

The Aesir were very pleased with their hostages but less pleased with their ruined walls. Then a stranger arrived at the gates of Asgard, offering to build a better defensive wall that could withstand any assault, and promising to have the work done within a year and a half. The offer seemed good to Odin—until he heard the price. The builder demanded in payment the sun, the moon, and marriage to Freya, who was quite unwilling to be married off. The rest of the gods and goddesses didn't want to see their city stripped of light and loveliness. But Odin feared an attack that would destroy that beauty forever.

After a long argument, the gods decided to accept the builder's offer, and his price, with one condition: that the builder work alone, that the wall be completed within one winter, and that the builder agrees to go unpaid if the work wasn't finished on time. Surely, they thought, the builder couldn't work so fast—but in pride and foolishness, he might overestimate his own capabilities, and so give them most of a wall free of charge. The gods rejoiced when the builder accepted the offer, and they willingly accepted his own condition—that his stallion Svadilfari should be allowed to help him haul stone for the wall. They swore all the oaths he asked of them, pledging to give him his price if he succeeded, and pledging that no god would hurt him while he worked on the wall. (This last promise was needed because of Odin's son Thor, the strongest and shortest-tempered of the gods. No one and nothing could stand against the terrible blows of Thor's thunder-hammer Mjöllnir, and Thor's power had not taught him anything about self-restraint. But even to Thor, an oath was an oath and could not be broken.)

But what a horse Svadilfari was! His speed, his strength, the stones he could move! He worked tirelessly, day and night, and three days before winter's end the building was done except for the gate. The wall was so high and strong that the gods couldn't pretend to be dissatisfied, and the work had gone so quickly that the gods never doubted it would be finished in time. They came together to debate the only question that remained: Which of them had had the terrible idea of accepting the builder's offer? They blamed the usual suspect in such cases: Loki.

Now Loki, the son of a giant, was perhaps the cleverest of the gods, though certainly not the wisest; he was full of ingenious ideas, and seldom took thought for their long-term consequences. He didn't deny that he'd made the suggestion, which had seemed brilliant to everyone else at the time. When they seized him and threatened him with torture and death if his suggestion led to their losing Freya and the light, he was terrified and swore to them that he would make sure the builder didn't complete the work. They let him go, trusting his oath to hold him, and also knowing that without his help they could see no way out of the bad bargain.

That night the builder went into the forest with his stallion to haul stone. He gloated in his heart, thinking of Freya, and also thinking of the rage and humiliation of the gods. He didn't notice the first time the mare whinnied in the depths of the wood. He didn't catch her scent on the wind. But Svadilfari did. He neighed, tossed his head, tore the lead from his master's hands and galloped into the darkness, chasing the mare who fled before him swiftly and silent as a shadow. The builder gave chase, shouting and cursing, but the horses left him far behind.

The builder, for all his strength and skill, couldn't carry the stone by himself. On the last day of winter, the gods pointed out that his work was unfinished, and he'd have to take himself off without pay. His fury was so fierce that it shattered his disguise, and he stood before them in his own form—a frost-giant, eager to harm the gods who had destroyed Ymir. Thor, seeing that, pulled out the thunder-hammer and struck the builder a blow that shattered him.

So the wall was built, and the gods kept Freya and the sun and moon. But the story of how the gods had cheated the giant spread far and wide, and it only deepened the hatred of the other frost-giants and their determination to take revenge. While the rest of the gods feasted and celebrated, Odin brooded about how and when that revenge would come.

But Loki, eleven months later, took a mare's shape again and gave birth to a fine strong foal, Svadilfari's son. The foal was a marvel, eight-legged and wonderfully strong and fast, and Odin rode him on his longest journeys.

Notes:

The tale of the war between the Aesir and the Vanir is told very briefly by Snorri Sturluson in the *Yngling Saga and* also, with some differences in detail, in *Skáldskaparmál*. For the building and the fortification of Asgard, I've mostly followed Snorri's tale in the *Gylfaginning* (see Notes to Chapter 1.). However, Snorri said that Asgard was the same city as Troy of the Greeks. Most commentators seem to think that was a later addition, and otherwise, the Greek and Norse stories don't seem to blend very well, so I've left that claim out.

Many of the Norse gods are shape-changers, appearing in god-form, or as mortal men and women, or as birds (often with the help of Freya's, or sometimes Frigg's, flight-feathers) or other animals. Loki the trickster, however, takes on an unusual number of shapes even for a Norse god, and this is the only story I know of which features a sex change as well as a species change.

I've used 'gods' here, as elsewhere in this book, to mean both male and female deities.

The physical layout and location of Asgard are rather puzzling. Snorri says, in the same tale, that Asgard is connected to the other worlds only by the rainbow bridge to prevent invasion; that it is Troy, and therefore a city in Midgard; and that it needed walls to keep giants at bay. The Poetic Eddas also offer baffling and apparently contradictory glimpses into where and what Asgard is.

Perhaps that is fitting—mortals are not able and are not intended, to fully understand the ways and workings of the gods.

Continue reading

Check out this book!

BIBLIOGRAPHY

Ancient Sources of Greek Myths:

Apollodorus [Pseudo-Apollodorus]. *The Library.* James George Fraser, trans. London: William Heinemann, Ltd., 1921.

Callimachus. *Hymns and Epigrams, Lycophron and Eratus.* A. W. Mair and G. R. Mair, trans. 2nd ed. Cambridge, Mass: Harvard University Press, 1921.

Hesiod. *Theogony and Works and Days.* M. L. West, trans. Oxford: Oxford University Press, 1988.

Homer. *The Iliad.* Robert Fagels, trans. New York: Viking Penguin, 1990.

———. *The Odyssey.* Robert Fagels, trans. New York: Viking Penguin, 1996.

Moore, Abraham, trans. *The Olympic and Pythian Odes of Pindar.* Boston: Nathan Haskell Dole, 1903.

Nagy, Gregory, trans. "Homeric Hymn to Demeter." <http://www.uh.edu/~cldue/texts/demeter.html> Accessed 12 February 2018.

Oldfather, C. H., trans. *Diodorus of Sicily in Twelve Volumes.* Volume 2: *Books II (continued), 35–IV, 58.* London: William Heinemann, Ltd., 1968.

Pausanias. *Description of Greece.* W. H. S. Jones, trans. Revised ed. Cambridge, MA: Harvard University Press, 1918.

Stewart, Aubrey, and George Long, trans. *Plutarch's Lives.* Vol. 1. London: G. Bell and Sons, 1925.

Modern Writings:

Haar, James. "Music of the Spheres." In *Oxford Music Online: Grove Music Online.* <www.oxfordmusiconline.com> Accessed 16 February 2018.

Wright, Craig. *The Maze and the Warrior: Symbols in Architecture, Theology, and Music.* Cambridge, MA: Harvard University Press, 2001.

Free Bonus from Captivating History (Available for a Limited time)

Hi History Lovers!

Now you have a chance to join our exclusive history list so you can get your first history ebook for free as well as discounts and a potential to get more history books for free! Simply visit the link below to join.

Captivatinghistory.com/ebook

Also, make sure to follow us on:

Twitter: @Captivhistory

Facebook: Captivating History:@captivatinghistory

www.ingramcontent.com/pod-product-compliance
Lightning Source LLC
Chambersburg PA
CBHW082107280426
43661CB00090B/929